THE
GOSPEL
OF
THOMAS

THE
GOSPEL
OF
THOMAS

WISDOM OF THE TWIN

A DYNAMIC TRANSLATION
WITH COMMENTARY AND NOTES

LYNN BAUMAN

WHITE CLOUD PRESS
ASHLAND, OREGON

I dedicate this text to the memory of
Marshall Voris, OSSJ,
and to a wise and wonderful being being,
Cynthia Bourgeault

First printing: 2002
Second printing: 2003

Cover Illustration by Carol Perry
Cover design by David Rupee
Printed in Malaysia

LIBRARY OF CONGRESS CATALOGING IN PUBLICATION DATA

Bauman, Lynn.
[Gospel of Thomas (Coptic Gospel). English]
The Gospel of Thomas : wisdom of the twin : a dynamic translation with
commentary and notes / Lynn Bauman.
p. cm.
Includes bibliographical references and index.
ISBN 1-883991-56-0 (pbk.)
1. Gospel of Thomas (Coptic Gospel)--Commentaries. I. Title.
BS2860.T5A3 2003
229'.8--dc22
2003022804

TABLE OF CONTENTS

Translator's Preface to
The Gosepl of Thomas

The translation of any text from one language to another is delicate business. This is especially true for the Coptic Gospel of Thomas, which is already a translation of an earlier Greek version. Moving between languages is never simple or easy. It requires agility as well as humility. Agility first in dealing with differing languages and the intellectual worlds and thought-forms they represent, but also humility as one approaches the text knowing that no one ever fully understands any language let alone the mind of a speaker in that language, nor is any translation ever adequate. My background in Middle Eastern thought and languages gives me a certain advantage as a translator, but I am continually humbled in this task by the realization that my attempts will always fall short of the power of the original.

The present translation you hold in your hand is called a "dynamic translation" in contrast to one that attempts to be perfectly literal, or one that is a wide-ranging paraphrase. This "middle ground" between these other two is territory not clearly marked, though most translators aim for it. Dynamic equivalency between languages, rather than direct word for word translation, requires that a word or phrase in one language be translated into its dynamic equivalent in the target language, so that the reader in the second language can feel the impact and meaning of the text in a way that is similar in the original version or to the first hearers of that text. This is, of course, complicated work. In Thomas we are already two languages removed from the original speaking of Jesus, so more ambiguity exists in it perhaps than is normal

My attempts have been to as accurately as possible reflect the power and nuance of the Coptic text, while recasting the language to make it compatible not only within the rules of modern English, but to its own flexible and dynamic nature. To some degree this requires that this translation, like all others, be an "interpretation" of the original.

A good example of what this means in practice is perhaps found in Logion 47 where the well-known statements about putting new wine into old wineskins is restated in contemporary English. We, of course, no longer use animal skins to store wine, at least in this part of the world. A dynamic equivalent in our world would be the following:

No one drinks a vintage wine and immediately wants to taste wine freshly bottled. New wine is not put into old containers lest it be ruined, nor is aged wine put into new barrels lest it spoil.

This phraseology translates the literal:

No one drinks aged wine and immediately want to drink new. New wine is not poured into old skins lest they split open, and aged wine is not put into fresh skins lest it be spoiled.

At other times, however, the meaning is far more ambiguous, and the interpretive decision-making is more precarious. What the Coptic language meant, let alone the original intention of the Greek text, is so distant that it is no longer possible to translate with any degree of certainty. In other cases there are multiple meanings and numerous ways to translate a text. Again, one has to make interpretive decisions. Hopefully in these cases what I have chosen accurately reflects at least one of the important meanings.

Many examples could be used to illustrate these particular aspects in the work of translation. Logion 27 is a good example. I have made the current translation to say,

If you do not fast from the cosmos, you will never grasp Reality. If you cannot find rest on the day of rest, you will never feast your eyes on God.

A more literal translation of the Coptic might be,

If you do not fast from the world you will never discover the Kingdom. If you cannot make the Sabbath, Sabbath, you will not see the Father.

Obviously a number of decisions had to be made about this particular text. One is to highlight in English the concept of fasting and feasting by using an English equivalent in the second part of the *Logion* for the verb "to see." "Feasting one's eyes on God" is that phrase. Several other decisions followed from this. The word Kingdom is problematic in modern English because it tends to narrow the concept to a political entity, when it clearly means more as a spiritual reality. To underscore this I have used different phrases to represent the word at alternative times (for example, divine Realm, divine Reality). The word "world" provides another example. Here I prefer to use the literal word from the Coptic text (*cosmos*) because it refers to more than just the world as a planet or a cultural entity. In place of the word "Father," which translates *Abba* from the first century language of Jesus referring to God both as Source and beloved parent, I have used other designations for deity. "Sabbath" (the day of rest) is also rendered here by its direct meaning so that it comes clearer to the modern ear. These decisions are all arbitrary to some degree, but in the interest of clarity and directness they seem appropriate to this translator. In addition to the one provided at the end of this volume, other excellent translations exist which are more literal. One can always compare this dynamic translation with these and reach a different conclusion. This, however, is not a paraphrase, where any liberty may be taken to make it more palatable to a modern audience. Again, I have tried to keep to some middle ground.

A final note concerning names and gender references needs to be made. In the translation the name **Yeshua** is used in place of Jesus. Yeshua is, of course, the original name for Jesus in Aramaic and Hebrew, which could also be translated as Joshua. Jesus is the Greek equivalent. Yeshua is chosen for this text to help shift our focus away from our conventional expectations of him to something potentially new.

Today we are quite aware of the need for of inclusive, gender neutral language. This requires that we work with languages and texts to produce pronouns for persons that, wherever possible, are fully inclusive. The original Coptic often refers by convention to "a man" when it means a person, either male or female. For example in Logion 2 the original text speaks about the one who must seek until "he" finds. To avoid this gender specific reference, the decision was made to change this and many similar constructions to "you" or "they" which eliminates this difficulty. Obviously this changes the text, but it is clear that Jesus is addressing persons directly, and "you" seems appropriate in many of these cases. Here again it is a translator's decision, and in the interest of its accessibility I have often chosen this course.

Throughout this task of translation I have been greatly assisted by the able work of Michael Grondin who has produced an on-line interlinear translation of the Coptic version of the Gospel of Thomas. Because as I began, Coptic was a new Near Eastern language for me, I have depended on his considerable efforts in learning the nuances of this particular language. Any error in my work, however, should not reflect on his important and careful study.

It is my hope that the present translation will spur deeper, more personal engagement with this ancient and powerful text. An extensive commentary based upon the same spiritual hermeneutic that has informed the translation is currently in progress. In addition, an academic translation with critical notes is also provided for scholars and students in this text for those who want to engage the critical issues and who wish also to know what decision were taken in translation and why.

Introduction to a Dynamic Translation of the Gospel of Thomas

Lynn C. Bauman

Jesus, the Master of Wisdom—an essential core lost to the West and replaced by Jesus, the object of dogma—has been recovered in the sands of Egypt. Over a half century ago, a full Coptic version of the "lost" Gospel of Thomas was discovered at Nag Hammadi among a collection of buried manuscripts. This Gospel, long known by name, but having disappeared from history, was recovered and translated by scholars causing great excitement and much consternation. It portrayed a very different Jesus from the one we have come to know through the centuries. The Gospel was also in a primitive form—a collection of *Logia* (also known as *Quelle*, German for Source)—the written expression of an oral tradition that had been suspected to exist prior to the writing of the canonical Gospels. In Thomas' Gospel, Jesus is presented as a Master of wisdom, dissimilar from the figure of dogma that was later to grow up around his memory. As in the traditional Gospels, he speaks with authority, but in Thomas his sayings are presented without the expected context of a story-line, the narrative supplied by Gospel writers.

A Plural Vision of Jesus

This short, cryptic text is made up of 114 sayings many of which were totally unknown before now. Those we recognize appear differently from their canonical counterparts, more spare and clean (some have described them as more "primitive," closer to their original source). The Coptic version is clearly a translation made much later after the original Greek (or perhaps early Aramaic) sayings were collected. According to textual scholars there is evidence of change, alternation, additions, deletions, and emendations by the hands of scribes as the collection passed through time and was

XII   THE GOSPEL OF THOMAS

ultimately constituted in the form discovered at Nag Hammadi, Egypt. Nonetheless, it represents something new for us, demonstrating what many were beginning to suspect and of which most scholars are now convinced, that the early Jesus-tradition was pluralistic—not monolithic as we had been led to believe in the West. Many views and visions of Jesus and his teachings sprang up around him and were promoted in different communities. Many "takes" on his life and its meaning existed from the start and were transmitted in various lineages across time spreading East and West from its original geographic homeland. In the modern West we happen to be heirs of one predominant strain preserved out of this multiplicity.

The sayings of Thomas (related to him at least in memory and by tradition), represent another strand, lost but loved by his students, preserving aspects of Jesus that present him as a sage and powerful teacher of Wisdom. But what is this wisdom? The answer to that question goes to the heart of the issues concerning this text. It is clear from a careful reading of Thomas that the wisdom tradition it expresses is quite different from the one preserved in the canonical Gospels, and also extends beyond the conventional wisdom of Israel. In it are strains of teaching that some see originating as far away as Taoist China, Buddhist Tibet, and Mazdean Persia in addition to the Hermetic, Pythagorean, and Mystery traditions of the Greeks, and the local but more important aspects of Jewish wisdom and its nascent mysticism.

THE "REAL" JESUS

Clearly precocious at age twelve (if the original canonical texts are to be believed), Jesus apparently never lost his curiosity and love of learning. A resident of Greek speaking Galilee, living in close proximity to the abundant flow of ideas and teachers (Jewish and foreign) which passed through that region, Jesus may have been privy to many spiritual influences current in the eastern Mediterranean of the first century. If the Gospel of Thomas is representative, he may also have absorbed vast amount of what he heard, synthesizing it into a new form according to some deep inner seeing. The protestation "Where did you get all this?" gives evidence of the shock that his non-traditional wisdom had on the ears of those who anticipated the expected. Thomas presents Jesus as a sage whose wisdom not only transcended local expectations, but was capable of grasping something far more universal than we have been led to believe.

Could this be the "real Jesus?" No amount of scholarship will ever settle the question once and for all. The Jesus we know, some feel, has been captured by institutions that have been reluctant to give up their version of him or see him in any other way but the forms accepted in the West. The Gospel of Thomas is therefore a threat, and yet, even in the structures through which he has been conventionally received, something of his brilliant sagacity and capacity to disturb shines through and continues to perplex us. Jesus was indeed a wise man. That, at least is clear. He spoke using aphorisms and parables, the hallmark of Hebrew wisdom preserved and transmitted for centuries. In fact, some of his early students declared that without the use of parables he spoke nothing at all. We have therefore never been fully deprived of his original wisdom, though what has often replaced it is a tamer version in the guise of a great moral teacher who later substitutes as vicar of heaven and judge of earth, wielding authority to save and condemn. But was he ever that? Thomas gives evidence that he was not.

QUESTIONS OF HISTORY AND TEXT

How, then, are we to understand Thomas and its origins? Is it authentic? Is it really Jesus we are hearing? Should these sayings be taken seriously by anyone today—be they Christian or non-Christian? In the modern western world there is deep uncertainty about how to answer these questions. We remain profoundly skeptical. Surrounded by a hermeneutic of suspicion, as all sacred texts now seem to be, Thomas has been hotly debated and variously interpreted, often dismissed or denounced by religious or scholarly authorities. Its authenticity was first called into question when its origination was first assigned to a late the second-century Gnostic community. After a half century of reflection and research, however, today's consensus is different. For many Thomas represents an authentic strain of the Jesus-tradition preserved by someone called Thomas, however altered it may have become during the ensuing centuries prior to its burial. In the meantime we are provided with a text that seems, perhaps providentially, to provoke and disturb all our neat categories and our carefully constructed Jesus.

So how are we to read Thomas? As a spurious, tangential text to the canonical documents officially accepted by Christianity, or as a new but essential addition to a core understanding of Jesus' teaching? The debate continues. It will likely be unending. There will perhaps never be a satisfactory resolution to these questions acceptable to all. How we answer them (the mystery of Thomas or the secret of Jesus) will depend to a large extent on the underlying presuppositions of those studying the texts. Textual scholarship and historical criticism can certainly help us better understand Thomas' words, but they can never provide absolute answers for many of the enigmas raised by its discovery. In the end each reader is forced to decide one way or another as to its personal significance and direct applicability. In the meantime, though, this ancient text should be read as a window that opens out upon a forgotten past that may help us recover a Jesus we never knew, but who has always existed.

A BRIEF HISTORY

Thomas was indeed found among a collection of primarily Gnostic documents, but there were other texts there as well. It was an eclectic library buried by monks when imperial Christianity demanded and got uniformity at all costs. Various versions of Christianity had persisted and flourished until, in later centuries, they were summarily suppressed or destroyed in the quest for dogmatic conformity. The tradition surrounding Thomas represents one strand of those early traditions preserved by the disciples of Thomas centered, it is felt, in the eastern regions of Syria outside the Empire. From there the followers of the Thomas tradition and their interpretation of Jesus spread further East and also South where it eventually found resonance among Coptic Christians, many of whom were influenced by Christian Gnostics. The Gospel of Thomas was clearly welcomed by them along with other writings, many from an earlier time including the Pauline Epistles and John's Gospel.

Eventually Thomas' Gospel was gathered into a library maintained by these monks. However, due to official pressure in the Empire to establish political uniformity and religious conformity, only certain ideas and texts were acceptable. All the rest were to be banned and burned, so the monks buried their precious trove of documents in jars, out of harms way, along the lower Nile valley banks where they remained hidden from prying eyes and the hands of the authorities until 1945.

READING THE TEXT

In order to read this text with understanding, we need certain tools, which must include, first, our awareness of the actors and figures behind the text and the traditions from which they speak. Second, we must also possess interpretive strategies that can assist us in discovering the many meanings of a collection that appears perhaps at first to be random and haphazard.

The tradition of wisdom that flows from Jesus is a complex one, far more complicated than the simplistic notions about him that we have often been taught. If these sayings represent an authentic picture of his wisdom, then his spiritual and intellectual world was indeed both interesting and complex. Furthermore, the wisdom of Jesus is not simply a repetition of the older stream of Hebrew thought faithfully repeated, but a fresh representation flowing from his own visionary seeing. Jesus is not simply passing on conventional wisdom. He seems to be synthesizing it; originating metaphoric material from personal insight that is powerfully and uniquely his own.

THE SOPHIOLOGY OF THOMAS

Many scholars suggest that the Gospel of Thomas represents a sophiology (a theology of wisdom) rather than a soteriology or a Christology (a theology of salvation through Christ, expressed in traditional Christian doctrine). As in Thomas, Jesus also speaks about finding the hidden treasure, and the pearl of great price in the canonical Gospels, but this is conventionally interpreted to mean that the disciple must find salvation from sin in this world through Christ. Although the Gospel of Thomas also expresses notions of redemption and restoration, it does not see these to be something external (a person is rescued by a "Savior" from without). Redemption, instead, has to do with finding the hidden treasure within. On this quest, the searcher is sent to discover the nature of his or her true Self, hidden and buried in a "field" on the inside. Discovery brings the student into the divine Realm.

Thomas places Jesus at the epicenter of this way of seeing and speaking, presenting him as the supreme sage, one of the *moshalim* (from the Hebrew word for parable, *mashal*), or teacher of wisdom. In the ancient lineage of the Hebrew people, of course, he follows in the tradition of Solomon, the wise king and progenitor of all Hebrew wisdom. But Jesus is also more than that. The text of Thomas'

Gospel presents itself, therefore, as a **theophany**, a divine self-disclosure, unveiling the inner secrets of the divine Reality disclosed to the eye of the heart of Jesus. His seeing conveys not only wisdom, but a visionary topography of the divine Realm (or kingdom) and its dimensions beyond the known world. As its expression or Word (*Logos*), Jesus becomes the "voice of the invisible," the conveyer of secrets and interpreter of the divine mysteries. In the cosmos (that complex of human and physical structures that make up the world), he is speaking for God.

MANY AUTHORS AND MULTIPLE LAYERS

Jesus, however, is not the only speaker. Some see him as a mere shadow figure, projected by Thomas the Twin, himself a clever interpreter of wisdom. Thomas is perhaps the same student who in the canonical Gospels struggled with the teachings and directives of Jesus. There he questioned everything, and doubted much. Could this be the one who eventually collected the "hard sayings" of Jesus, those which escaped the notice of the rest of the Apostles simply because they were too obscure? Thomas became the guide into these mystery teachings, and now he stands at the gate, at the head of the stream, as the authenticator of a later community of students gathered around him forming a way of life in the eastern lands of early Christianity modeled on their teachings.

Scholars posit that it is not only Thomas, but the whole Syrian community that treasures and transmits these sayings, shaping the collection until it eventually reaches the community of Coptic monks. Many speakers, many hands and voices, transmit the sayings and claim that they are the "authentic words of Jesus." But are they? We will never know for certain. What we do know now is that by comparison the way in which they appear in Thomas seems to be less formed and more primitive, closer to the original, than the sayings preserved in the canonical Gospels. Many now believe that indeed we are touching an early, less well known source of the original teachings of Jesus.

VISIONARY TOPOGRAPHY

Understanding the Gospel of Thomas in the modern world requires that we use a spiritual hermeneutic or interpretive strategy known to the ancients and grounded in their understanding of its visionary topography. For them heaven and earth (the "book-ends" of their cosmology) was dense with realities that can only be expressed symbolically. Without knowing this topography one cannot help but read Thomas in an exterior way, as a literary document. The opening *Logia*, however, demand an interior reading based upon an interpretation that will eclipse the obvious and the apparent, in order that a hidden reality may appear. Clues to that topography and the strategy for interpretation may be gained from a careful reading of the text itself, but various forms of traditional wisdom, whose source is the ancient Middle East, make that topography explicit, namely the ascent codes of Jewish Merkavah mysticism and the angelology of the Persians.

The visionary topography in Thomas could best be defined by the relationship between time and eternity, or the finite and the Infinite—also described as the relationship between heaven and earth. The juxtaposition of these two realms situates a third realm, namely the kingdom, from whose reality we are said to spring prior to our physical arising. It is territory that can only be known now through search and the return journey of personal participation. The kingdom exists as a sacred geography between the Alpha and the Omega of temporality. In this in-between land, the Kingdom of God unfolds at the juncture where time and eternity meet. It is constituted by multiple domains and dimensions that link the cosmos together in a totality called "the All" (*ta panta*). What is also crucial for our understanding is to know that Jesus understands this realm also to exist within. It is an inner domain as well in which a new, transcendent reality unfolds.

INNER ALIGNMENT

The Gospel of Thomas is perfectly aligned to this realm, which is perhaps best expressed as a parallel universe transcendent to, but inclusive of, the temporal and spatial order that we inhabit as well as the spiritual dimensions that dwell within us. This topography, therefore, is no mere abstraction. It is a specific region (*topos*) composed of non-local and non-temporal coordinates—in short, a landscape whose dimensions and domains stretch as an isthmus between the chasm of Ultimate Reality and temporality, through which all must pass on their pilgrimage of exile and return. Regardless of whether Thomas heard and faithfully transmitted this wisdom directly from Jesus, an understanding of its cosmological contours is determinative for a comprehensive understanding of the text. Without orientation to its topography and unique angle of vision, Thomas makes little sense. With it, however, the text is saturated with meaning.

In Thomas Jesus speaks from a timeless, universal place of seeing—from a perception that calls humanity to awaken to its own inner reality. He calls each of us to the light within all things that blazed forth at the beginning from the Father's presence before the soul we are, created outside of time, first donned the body's shirt and fell into the density of space-time—the shadow of God's love. And yet it is here in space and time, within the depths of the cosmos, that we can come to know the true Self, and the truth about ourselves. It is here we can awaken, stand up on our own feet and become a unified being—no longer two but one—aligned to and a participant in the deep magnetic axis of Ultimate Reality conjoined to the inner spiritual axis of the human heart and consciousness.

Working deep in the river of the world's events, Jesus as Awakener to what is hidden in the wisdom-field of the heart appears as the Voice of that Presence that has surrounded us and been seeking us from the beginnings of our terrestrial exile. He will not rest until the cosmos is set ablaze with fire and humanity is released into the light, alive with the pain of the longing for return. For we have come from a country, a kingdom beyond this universe, the cosmos. And yet knowledge of our origins has been stolen from us. We believe we are one thing, but we are in truth another. We search the world for satisfaction to the hunger and thirst within, knocking on the outer doors of material and social reality for the answer, when in truth the answer lies buried, concealed within.

Fire and light as witness to this Reality, eventually makes our longing strong enough to bring us at last to hear the voice of the clarifying Presence whose task it is to help us discover the treasure hidden in the heart. And when we find it, the truth of it, and the truth about ourselves, we slip free of the bindings that hold us and stand naked before the One whose Presence floods us with the original light. At that moment we can begin to discern the Face of the One whose love and compassion has always known us and pursued us across the fierce landscape of our exile. As we surrender to this Guide, hearing and obeying his voice,

we transcend ourselves and come to know this as the meaning behind all things and of our own existence. At the end (which is also
the beginning), the hidden treasure is finally known "on earth as it
is in heaven," and the veil dividing heaven and earth, Creator and
creature, Knower and known is stripped away and we are revealed
for who we truly are.

A STRATEGY FOR READING THOMAS

Reading Thomas' Gospel in this light it is quite clear that we are
in a world significantly different from the traditional, canonical
Gospels, but is such a reading justified? As was noted earlier, Thomas is a collection of separate (and some would say disjointed) sayings, whereas the traditional Gospels form a coherent storyline
across time. This raises, of course, the issue of unity. Is this simply a
collection of disparate sayings without inner consistency or coherence? If one concludes it does have unity, then what is that unity,
and how does one discern the structure that makes the teaching of
Jesus in these sayings coherent? Finally, what is the interpretive criteria (the hermeneutical lens) by which the wisdom of these sayings
may be understood and its life-giving qualities revealed?

Some, of course, see little or no unity at all in Thomas—its existence is merely the result of multiple layerings made by many collectors, authors, and compilers across time. While there is indeed evidence of an evolution of this text into a final form, there is also evidence that the Gospel of Thomas, at whatever stage in its development, was understood even by its compliers to be coherent, but a
coherence different from what we might imagine. Surprisingly, perhaps its coherence must be completed by someone other than the
collectors or compilers themselves. Because Thomas has little or no
narrative context, the structure of Thomas is of an entirely different
type from that of the canonical Gospels. The contrast might be expressed as the difference between the diachronic narratives of Matthew, Mark, Luke and John (which move across a historical landscape in time, punctuated by events and personal exchanges) and
the synchronic structure of Thomas (whose sayings are narrated se-
quentially but whose meanings are ultimately synchronous).

Despite what some allege, the relationship of these sayings does
not seem to be haphazard; the collection is not chaotic nor are the
sayings randomly gathered. Upon careful examination, it appears
that Thomas has juxtaposed the *Logia* in a particular sequence to cre-

ate an interpretive framework of synchronic significance. Each saying is intentionally linked by meaning and content to the one (or ones) before and after it. Often these connections are word repetitions, metaphoric resonances, or parallel thought structures (similar to those found in the Psalms).

THE JOURNEY OF INTERPRETATION

If the narrative arrangement of the canonical Gospels is replaced in Thomas with a synchronic structure, then semantic connection between sayings must be accomplished by a method other than historical chronology. That means is situated within readers themselves. To be a coherent teaching, the context must be supplied by the careful reading and spiritual awareness of one who reads—otherwise the sayings do fall into hopeless chaos. One crucial strategy for providing such a context is to understand these sayings as part of an inner dialogue of question and answer. As they are read, questions are inevitably raised by the sayings themselves in the mind of the reader. Each saying suggests a relevant question (or questions) that will need to be answered if the meaning of that saying is to be understood and fully lived. The "logic" between sayings is therefore that later sayings (or sets of sayings) will answer a question (or questions) raised earlier. Each saying is synchronically referential and consubstantial. One saying, therefore, is not joined chronologically to the next through narrative or history, but semantically through meaning. The meanings that came before and the those which come after are crucial for understanding each separate *logion* and, ultimately, the meaning of the entire text.

The sayings, however, are also semantic worlds unto themselves. Each *logion*, therefore, is like a small world held within larger worlds of meaning, each one forming an integral part of the total Gospel that constitutes the whole, representing the cosmic vision that Jesus, the Seer and Teller of Parable knows. In reading the Gospel, the associations of meaning between sayings endlessly reverberate across the entire landscape of the text, transmuting correspondences into synchronic states which more and more amplify the overall meaning. Truth, as a form of traditional wisdom, read and understood in this way has the ability to penetrate the heart, creating "states of soul," by which a receptive reader and the symbolic meaning of the sayings harmonize in the coincidence of the reader's experience. This synchronicity of symbol and soul becomes the spiritual configuration of a precise inner reality that is the work of a student and the teaching of a living Master of wisdom.

Eventually the resonances between the *Logia* build up into a kind of musical harmony, which is orchestrated by the personal participation and perception of the reader as he or she unravels specific meaning in the context of the entire Gospel. Through such participation the reader is able to transfigure the words into images, and images into symbols, interpreting the cosmological and spiritual dimensions of the text. This method illustrates what the French oriental scholar, Henry Corbin, describes as "a hermeneutic of progression" whereby the transfiguration of the written material from a sacred text into spiritually potent metaphors and symbols becomes, itself, a journey of the soul. The determination of meaning as the exegesis of text is itself an exodus—the ascent and return of the soul from the world of exile towards its origin and home (Corbin, 1998, 160).

PRACTICAL APPLICATIONS AND PERSONAL LEARNING

Fundamentally, Thomas is a collection of sayings that has practical, as well as spiritual value. The Gospel itself begins with the promise that one who discerns the meaning of these words will not taste (experience in practice) death. So understanding and experience are causally linked in these opening statements. Inevitably meaning must give way to practice. In order to understand one must live what one reads. As one engages each saying, the immediate question, "What does it mean?" leads to other questions which imply issues of practice, "How does one do this, live this, or follow these injunctions?" Thomas, therefore, is also a primordial text of spiritual practice. The questions raised by its instructions guide us to answers that are logically apparent only if one were to live them out.

It is through such an interpretive journey that one emerges at the end of the text with a Gospel in hand, not one narrated by Thomas from without, but by the reader from within. In point of fact, the text is literally said to be a Gospel (a text proclaiming Good News) only at its conclusion, after the reader has made the journey of interpretation, and not at the beginning, as was normal for the other Gospels. When the reader has created a personal narrative out of the meanings gleaned from the text and woven them practically into life, only then can it be said that Thomas is a Gospel. And in the end, as Jesus will say, the reader/interpreter is "standing up" vertically in the cosmos with the taste of life having arisen from a position of horizontal death.

In whatever century it is read, then, the Gospel of Thomas is an invitation to interpretive work. It requires our participation now in the modern world just as it did in the ancient world in order to unlock its secrets and deliver its promise of life. Then, and only then does it become "Good News" passing through the ages from the lips of one who was anointed with Spirit, possessing the wisdom to proclaim it.

A Reader's Guide to
The Gospel of Thomas

Dialogical Exchange and the Missing Narrative

Within the streams of wisdom coming to us from the ancient traditions of the Middle East, there is the repeated theme —seek and you will find. This theme also reappears in the opening lines of the Gospel of Thomas. These words raise important questions for all seekers of wisdom—how does one seek and where does one find?

Both in content and in form the Gospel of Thomas attempts to answer to these questions. Not only does it provide a corpus of understanding, the search for wisdom also involves a methodology augmented by the very structure of the text itself. Thomas, which calls itself a "gospel" only at the end, is unlike the conventional texts of the Gospels we are used to. Matthew, Mark, Luke and John are well-formed narratives—telling a story recounted in the first century of the Common Era. Thomas is unlike them. It exists in a more "primitive" form, as a collection of *logia* in the "sayings tradition" of early Christianity. Some have said that this collection is randomly assembled with little rhyme or reason. But is it? Might its apparent disorder be part of its teaching, and its lack of narrative structure a hidden strategy to instruct the seeker of wisdom by a means we are not used to? Many now believe (this author included) that not only are we faced with one of the streams of first-century wisdom originating in Jesus, at least in part, but we are also invited into a method of instruction intrinsic to the tradition of wisdom both then and now.

This system of teaching often "hidden" to the modern mind because it utilizes stratagems so unlike our contemporary pedagogies, forces our hand, challenges our minds, and opens us to wisdom in a new and different way. To gain understanding from this text it is necessary to create our own personal narrative arising from dialogical inquiry. Known as the Socratic method in the West, this way of pursuing wisdom seems basic to the text itself. To understand Thomas, it is important to engage the text in a dialogical way. Forced by the missing narrative, the reader must also become the "gospeler" creating a unique, personal narrative, as Thomas will say, by engaging the "living Jesus" in dialogue through its sayings.

As a reader of this text, your strategy for determining meaning, therefore, can also be dialogical. As you endeavor to understand each saying, issues and questions will naturally arise. If this Socratic approach is correct, subsequent sayings will answer at least some of your questions and concerns. Not all questions, of course, will. For some of them there may never be a resolution, but if you stay open and alert, many important ones will be answered. This translation and reader's guide takes this strategy (the question and answer method in Socratic dialogue) seriously. Because this methodology may be new or unfamiliar to you, this text has been written in a particular way. To assist you in dialogical exchange, a set of **questions for reflection** rising naturally from the text itself is provided after each saying. Using these questions, you can explore the *logia*, and in that way engage the **Wisdom of the Twin** in dialogue. You may need, of course, to add new questions to each list as you go. It is important that you take notes on what you find and the insights you gain. Make a journal of your discoveries. This is an important part of the methodology in the study of wisdom.

DISCOVERING THE META-STRUCTURE OF THOMAS

One can imagine that there may be some over-arching "meta-structure" to the Gospel of Thomas that would become clearer as one became familiar with the meaning of each individual saying. In the philosophical language of interpretation theory (the study of hermeneutics) such a structure is known as the "semiotics of the text"—that is, the self-referential way in which the text hangs together on its own terms without reference to other, outside sources. Based upon a careful reading of the Gospel of Thomas it does indeed appear to have its own unique semiotic structure. It holds together, but in a strange way, only after the dialogical method of inquiry has been employed by the reader.

As was pointed out in the Introduction, the structure is not a plotline tied to a temporal history, as in the canonical Gospels. It is more "symphonic" than that. The beauty of a piece of orchestral music is complete only when each part adds its voice to the whole — it is then that we hear the full majesty of the music. In like manner, each saying plays a role in the totality of the whole, and as in an orchestra, a note in one section of the text, may parallel (or resonate with) with notes in other sections. Pay close attention, therefore, to parallel or repeating images and concepts, matching metaphors, and the echo of ideas finding resonance across the text. As you read and study the *logia* look for connections. It might be helpful to draw diagrams, flow charts, and arrows from one saying to another.

An illustration of what you might experience is the "magic eye" technique of seeing the hidden picture in a riot of surface colors and dots. After paying a special kind of attention before this confusion of color and form a coherent image can be seen to "stand up" out of the page in three-dimensional form. This same experience seems to be one known by many who have given their full attention to wisdom texts and teachings presented in aphoristic and parabolic ways.

The "hidden" meaning of this text only appears when the disorder of multiple images, metaphors, words, and evocations are coordinated by attending to some new or higher coherence. One, however, can never see this clearer image (or grasp its meaning) until one's full attention has been brought to bear. Sustained observation and concentration will increase the possibility that wisdom herself will appear in the form of divine Theophany or encounter.

LOGION 1

I who write this am Thomas,
the Double, the Twin.
Yeshua, the Living Master spoke,
and his secret sayings I have
written down.

I assure you, whoever grasps their
meaning will not know the taste
of death.

Academic Translation

These are the hidden sayings which the living Yeshua spoke, and I Didymos Judas Thomas (the Twin) wrote them down. He says, whoever discovers the meaning of these words will not take a taste of death.

Notes

a. Reference to "the Twin" is signified by both names, **Didymous** (which means twin in Greek), as well as **Thomas** (which is the Semitic form).

b. The name **Yeshua** is the original name of Jesus in Aramaic and Hebrew. It is kept in both translations (the dynamic and academic versions) to enhance the sense of Yeshua's Semitic origins.

c. The word **says** is a direct translation of the present tense used in fragments of the Gospel of

NOTES

The material following the dynamic translation provide 1) a series of Questions for Reflection, 2) an academic translation of the Gospel of Thomas, and 3) explanatory notes relating to translation issues. These notes relate first of all to the dynamic version, and then secondarily to the academic version. Without being stilted or overly formal, the academic version of this text seeks to preserve aspects of the original Coptic text that are important for those doing further research and study. Words, phrases, or terms in bold indicate wording in the dynamic version, while words in "parenthesis" designate those appearing in the academic version or the original text.

QUESTIONS FOR REFLECTION

1. This first saying implies that you already know the taste of death. What does death taste like? In your own experience how might you have tasted death? How would you describe its taste? What would it mean (or be like) not to taste death?
2. If grasping the meaning of the words in the Gospel of Thomas will result in not knowing the taste of death, then how does one discover (or seize upon) the meaning of these words? What would one have to do (or be) in order to interpret a wisdom text?
3. Because the name Thomas (which means "the Twin") is repeated twice, once in Greek and once in Aramaic, it appears to be important for the text itself. If it is not simply a name (the name of the one who has collected and compiled this Gospel), then what might be its sophiological (wisdom) significance? What is the meaning of "twin?" How might it be a kind of code word expressing a truth in the wisdom tradition? Keep this question open and alive all the way to the end. Try to reflect on it

Thomas found earlier called the Oxyrynchus Papyrii. It will be used in the dynamic translation, but not in the academic. The original Coptic text expresses it in the past tense. The present tense emphasizes the immediacy of the text and the speaking of Jesus.

d. In these opening lines, the direct referent to the one speaking (**I assure you...**) could certainly be Jesus. However, it is more likely Thomas who is giving us this briefest of instructions on how to interpret the text.

e. The term **grasps** (or "discovers") literally means to fall upon or seize, as one would some precious object on the ground that one might lose otherwise. This key term will be repeated thirty-

throughout your inquiry of the text. You may find answers to this question at many points in your study of this Gospel, and these may prove to be important clues.

4. Who is Yeshua as portrayed by this text? How is he the same or different from the person of Jesus you may have known previously? Why is he called the Living One, and why might these sayings be his "secret" (or hidden) sayings? All these questions may not be answered immediately, but they should form the backdrop for more specific questions each saying raises.

Personal Reflections

one times through out the entire manuscript. The word **meaning** *could be rendered "interpretation."*

Logion 2

Yeshua says,

If you are searching,
    you must not stop
    until you find.
When you find, however,
you will become troubled.
Your confusion will give way to wonder.
In wonder you will reign over all things.
Your sovereignty will be your rest.

Acdemic Translation

Yeshua said, "Let not the one(s) seeking stop until they find. But when they find they will become troubled. Trouble will give place to wonder, in which they will reign over the All, (and their sovereignty will be their rest)."

Notes

a. The masculine pronoun "he" in the original text has been translated typically as **you** *in the dynamic version (or sometimes "the one" or "ones" in the academic translation). The purpose is to maintain the aspiration of inclusive language important for the modern ear.*

b. The terms **trouble** *and* **confusion** *translate the same word in the original. The words* **all things** *trans-lates a specific phrase that in*

QUESTIONS FOR REFLECTION

1. This opening **logion,** which is perhaps the foundation for every journey of discovery within the wisdom tradition, sets the stage for what is to follow. Notice that these instructions coming from Hebrew wisdom, spell out the conditions for grasping the meaning of the sayings and for becoming a wise person.
2. Six conditions are mentioned. What do they mean? Clearly defining these words is important for a deeper understanding of this Gospel.
3. Where do these six conditions appear in the rest of the text? (You will want to be looking for them).
4. If the conditions for grasping the meaning of the secret sayings of Yeshua are active, where might they lead?
5. Where should you begin your search? What would be the criteria by which you might discern whether or not you were starting at the right place to discover the hidden meaning? What is the right place to begin such an inquiry?

Personal Reflections

*Greek (***pas,** *or* **ta panta***) was used as a cognate for the Semitic concept of the Kingdom and is found extensively in the writings of St. Paul.*

c. The phrase **your sovereignty will be your rest** *is not found in the Coptic translation from which this text comes. It is, however, recorded in the Greek Oxyrynchus fragment believed to be an earlier version. This phrase, therefore, is added in conformity with that earlier text.*

d. Both **reign** *and* **sovereignty** *translate the words "become king" found in the Coptic text.*

LOGION 3

Yeshua says,

If your spiritual guides say to you,
   "Look, the divine Realm is
      in the sky,"
well then the birds
will get there ahead of you.
If they say,
"It is in the sea,"
then the fish will precede you.

No, divine Reality exists
inside and all around you.
Only when you have come to know your
true Self will you be fully known—
realizing at last that you
are a child of the Living One.
If, however, you never come to know
who you truly are,
you are a poverty-stricken being,
and it is your "self"
which lies impoverished.

Academic Translation

Yeshua said, "If those leading you say to you, 'Look, the Kingdom is in the sky!' Well, then, the birds of the sky will precede you. If they say, 'It is in the sea,' then the fish will get there ahead of you. No, the divine Realm is inside and all around you. When you come to know your self, you will be known, and you will realize that you are the sons (and daughters) of the Living Father. If, however, you do not know your self, then you live impoverished, and you yourself are that poverty."

Notes
a. This is the first instance where the Coptic word for "the kingdom" is translated with a cognate term, **Realm** *or* **Reality**. *The word* **realm** *translates "kingdom" in the original text and in the academic*

QUESTIONS FOR REFLECTION

1. According to this logion, what is the goal of searching and finding in the wisdom tradition? Is it merely to find something new or different from what you already know? What would be the result of finding?
2. What is the true Self in contrast to its opposite—the false self? You may have heard these terms used before. What do they seem to mean here?
3. What is an impoverished self? In what forms do impoverishment (or poverty) come in your world? Is this condition experienced by most people, or just the poor of the earth? Have you experienced poverty or impoverishment? If so, how?
4. How would one go about getting to know the true Self? Where might you find out about the nature of your own true Self?

version. In English it is a more expansive, inclusive and politically neutral word. It identifies its referent as a domain, a reality which is ultimate and transcendent to all else that we know.

b. The term **divine** *(or God's) is added to identify this realm as the Kingdom of God (or alternatively, the Kingdom of heaven) which is the subject of much of Yeshua's teaching.*

c. The word **sky** *is also the word for heaven in Coptic.*

d. **All around you** *(or outside you) in the original text is related to the seeing-eye. However this wording in the original may be due to scribal error because of the similarity of* **eye** *to* **outside** *in Coptic.*

e. The words **true Self** *are used here to express specific meaning as it unfolds across the text of the Gospel of Thomas.*

f. **Child of the Living One** *translates the gender specific "sons of the living Father." Gender specificity, however, is expressed by convention and restricts the more comprehensive inclusivity that is expressed here and throughout the entire text. However, expressing it this way in an inclusive language translation, may prohibit the immediacy of recognizing that one belongs intimately to a particular parentage. One should be able to say, "I belong to God. God is my Father (or Mother, as Jesus will also say later in the text).*

g. **Poverty-stricken being** *is literally "you exist in poverty."*

Personal Reflections

Logion 4

Yeshua says,

A person of advanced age
must go immediately and
ask an infant born just
seven days about life's source.
Such asking leads to life
when what is first becomes last.
United they become a single whole.

Academic Translation

Yeshua said, "An individual of many days will not delay in asking an infant child, seven days old, about the source of life, and will live. For many who are first will be last, and they will become a single whole."

Notes

a. The term **source** *translates the Greek word* **topos** *which means the location, ground, dwelling place, or seat. In this sense it represents both the source and origin, as well as the place of destiny – or the place to which one's life or destiny leads. It is also the word from which we get topography.*

b. **A single whole** *is literally "one alone." This phraseology concerns the concept of* **unity** *or* **oneness** *which is a constant theme expressed throughout this collection of Logia.*

QUESTIONS FOR REFLECTION

1. What is the meaning of these strange metaphors used by Yeshua? Why do you think he is using them?
2. Who is this person of "advanced age?"
3. Who is the "infant born just seven days?"
4. What is the significance of the number seven here, or is it simply arbitrary?
5. What and where is "life's source?"
6. What is the meaning of the words "when what is first becomes last?" If you were to draw a diagram to illustrate this image, what might the picture be?
7. If you compare the previous "taste of death" (Logion 1) with the form of life spoken about in this saying, what would the contrast be?
8. Significant numerations are also found in the last phrase. How would you write out the numbers suggested here?
9. How does the aged person ask the infant and get the answer? Who is this "infant?" Is it any infant?
10. Where might you go to ask the infant the question about life's source?

Personal Reflections

LOGION 5

Yeshua says,

Come to know the One
in the presence before you,
and everything hidden
from you will be revealed.
For there is nothing concealed
that will not be revealed,
and nothing buried
that will not be raised.

Academic Translation

Yeshua said,
"Know the One in the Presence before your face, and what is hidden from you will be revealed. For there is nothing hidden that will not appear, (and nothing buried that will not be raised)."

QUESTIONS FOR REFLECTION

1. In this saying it is important to note that **hidden** is actually the same word as **secret**, referring back to the first words in this Gospel about the secret sayings of Yeshua.
2. The opening words of this logion are interesting because there is more than one entity involved. How many "persons" or "presences" are actually drawn into this knowing?
3. What is the significance of a "presence" and "One in the presence?"
4. It might be important to note that the words "before you" could also be rendered "right in front of your face." What would these phrases actually mean in experience?
5. How would one get to know the One who fills the presence? What would the effect of such knowing be?
6. The promise made in this saying is twofold. What does it mean? Does it suggest a future state of any kind? Who (or what) is being revealed and raised?

Personal Reflections

Notes

a. Another possible translation of the opening segment of this text is: "(Learn to) recognize what is present right in front of your face."

b. The word **hidden** is the same word used to describe the "hidden sayings" of Jesus at the beginning of the text.

c. The final phrase is found in the Greek fragment, the Oxyrynchus Papyrus, and seems to have been present in at least one of the early Greek manuscripts.

LOGION 6

His students asked him,

Do you want us to fast?
          How shall we pray?
          Should we give offerings?
From what foods must we abstain?"

Yeshua answered,

"Stop lying.
Do not do what you hate,
because everything here lies open
before heaven.
Nothing hidden will remain secret,
for the veil will be stripped away from
all that lies concealed behind it."

Academic Translation

His students asked him, "Do you want us to fast? How shall we pray? Should we give alms? From what foods must we abstain?" Yeshua said, "Do not lie, and do not do what you hate, for these things are revealed before the presence of heaven. Nothing hidden will not appear and nothing covered up will remain concealed."

Questions for Reflection

1. Notice that the list of questions his students ask are the concerns of any practicing Jew. Naturally his religious students would want to know Yeshua's answers to these standard questions about religious duty and piety.
2. Like many others found in Thomas and in the canonical Gospels, Yeshua's answer transcends the literal level of their questions and propels them toward a deeper issue. How does Yeshua's answer move to the heart of the question of religious practice or piety? What would be the crucial importance of these two negatives for spiritual practice?
3. What does it mean to stop lying, or doing what you hate?
4. What is the opposite to the negative strategy suggested here?
5. What do lying and doing what you hate create inside a human being?
6. What is the rationale for changing one's behavior? Are the reasons given for abstaining from these human actions of any value in the modern world, or have we moved beyond this kind of external motivation?

Personal Reflections

Notes

a. In the Coptic text the words translated as "everything lies open before heaven" is the term "in the presence of heaven," also found in the previous saying.

LOGION 7

Yeshua says,

A lion eaten by a man is blessed
as it changes to human form,
but a human devoured
by a lion is cursed
as lion becomes human.

Academic Translation

Yeshua said, "Blessed is the lion which becomes human when eaten by a man, but cursed is the man which a lion eats and the lion becomes human."

QUESTIONS FOR REFLECTION

1. In order to begin to understand this paradoxical saying, it should first be noted that the word **blessed** is the same one used in the beatitudes of the canonical Gospels. Second, the two parts of this saying are not parallel or symmetrical. This is what makes the saying confusing to the logical mind.
2. Who is the lion-eating man, why is he blessed and how is he blessed?
3. How does one "eat the lion?" How does a lion eat a man? What do these metaphors mean?
4. What is blessing in the first instance, and cursing in the second? In what form do these come?
5. If the lion becomes human in both cases, then what is the difference between them?
6. Try making a diagram of this **logion**. See if the diagram can help you understand the metaphors better. Are there any spatial characteristics inherent in this saying that helps to clarify what is happening?

Personal Reflections

Notes

a. In the Coptic text the term **a man** *has the definite article "the man" which may refer to the concept of the archetypal human, which is often understood to be the meaning behind the phrase Son of Man, used by Jesus as a title for himself within the canonical Gospels.*

LOGION 8

Yeshua says,

A true human being can be compared to a wise fisherman who casts his net into the sea and draws it up from below full of small fish. Hidden among them is one large, exceptional fish that he seizes immediately, throwing back all the rest without a second thought. Whoever has ears let them understand this."

Academic Translation

Yeshua said, "A human being can be compared to a wise fisherman who casts his net into the sea. He drew it up from out of the sea full of small fish, and discovered among them a great, good fish. Choosing the great fish without any difficulty, the wise fisherman threw all the rest back into the sea. Whoever has ears to hear let them listen."

Notes

a. The **one large, exceptional fish** *is literally said to be both "great" (large) and "good." This second term indicates quality, that which makes it* **exceptional.** *All the rest of the fish are called "little ones" perhaps indicating both size and quality.*

QUESTIONS FOR REFLECTION

1. If you were to make a diagram for the actions occurring in this saying similar to the one for Logion 7, how might the two pictures be related? In both cases there are spatial relationships that appear to be symbolic.
2. How are the previous logia and this one related?
3. What is the definition of a "true human being" according to the wisdom of this saying?
4. In the metaphoric world of this saying there are many elements: a fisherman, a net, a sea, small fish, a large fish. In addition there are multiple forms of action: casting, drawing up, seizing, throwing back, thinking. All of these symbolic elements work together to transmit the wisdom of this logion. How would you incorporate them all into a single, cohesive unit?
5. What is the large fish? What does it stand for? Where does it come from? What is the significance of its size?
6. What makes this person wise?
7. How do these fishing metaphors relate to the next logion which uses agricultural language, both favorites in the teaching of Yeshua?

Personal Reflections

LOGION 9

Yeshua says,

A farmer went out to plant,
seed in hand he scattered
it everywhere.
Some fell on the surface of the road.
Birds came and ate it.
Other fell on rocky ground
and could not take root in the earth,
or send grain heavenward,
and so never germinated.
Still other seed fell among
weeds and brambles which
choked it out and insects devoured.
Some, however, fell onto fertile soil
which produced fruit of high quality
yielding as much as sixty and
one-hundred and twenty percent.

Academic Translation

Yeshua said, "Behold, a sower came out, filled his hand with seeds, and scattered them everywhere. Some fell on the road, but birds came and ate them. Others fell among rocks, but they did not take root in the earth nor send their heads rising to the sky. Other seed fell among thorns which choked them, and insects devoured them. Some seed did fall on good earth which sent abundant fruit heavenward yielding sixty and a hundred and twenty-fold."

QUESTIONS FOR REFLECTION

1. In this saying (like the one above it) there are multiple metaphors and actions. Once again, in order to understand its meaning, you might diagram or picture the action using the metaphors to give you clarity.
2. Is the actor in this logion the same or different from the actor in the previous saying?
3. What ground (with its multiple conditions) is this saying referring to? These pictures are very important because they describe states and conditions which human beings are or experience.
4. What is the seed sown and what is its quality in relationship to the kinds of ground upon which it falls?

Personal Reflections

Notes

a. Twice in this logion the grain is said to be sent "rising to the sky" or "heavenward," emphasizing a particular direction or destination for what it is being produced. The actual phrase is "it gave fruit up to the sky."

LOGION 10

Yeshua says,

See, I have sown fire into the cosmos, and I shall guard it carefully until it blazes.

Academic Translation

Yeshua said, "I have cast fire into the cosmos, and look, I am watching over it until it is blazes."

QUESTIONS FOR REFLECTION

1. The relationship between this saying and the previous one is very interesting. What question from those raised earlier does it appear to answer?
2. In your judgment is the image of fire used here negative or a positive?
3. How would you define the cosmos into which this fire has been thrown?
4. Why do you imagine Yeshua is guarding it so carefully?
5. What might happen when the fire blazes up?

Personal Reflections

Notes

a. The term **cosmos** *is the actual Greek word used in the Coptic text. Its meanings in first-century Greek are diverse. Certainly it stands for the seen and unseen universe, but in the Christian Scriptures it appears to have specific reference to the world of human creation usually under-stood to be predominated by negative forces.*

b. The term **guard** *or "watch over" is used in Logion 79 where it also has the meaning of a more active intention to "keep" or even, "practice."*

LOGION 11

Yeshua says,

The sky and all that lies in the dimensions above it will cease to exist.

The dead know nothing of life,
and the living will never die.

When you consume that which is
already dead, you are turning it back
into life.

So, then, when you too emerge
back into the Light,
what will you do?

For on the day when you
were created one,
you also became two,
but when you come to realize your
twoness again,
what will you do?

Academic Translation

Yeshua said, The sky and the heaven above it will pass away. Those who are dead live not and the living will not die. In the days when you were eating what was dead you were making it alive. When you come to be in the light, what will you do? On the day when you were one, you were made two, but when you come to be two, what will you do?

Notes

a. In the Coptic text there are two parallel grammatical constructions in this saying difficult to detect in any translation that seem also to suggest parallel or related ideas. The first parallel construction has to do with making (or creating something). It is expressed as **turning it back into life** *and* **when you were created one, you**

QUESTIONS FOR REFLECTION

1. This is a collection of sayings that Thomas brings together into a unit. At first glance they appear to be unrelated, but in his mind, at least, they were united. What is the connection between them? One strategy might be to start not only at the top of his list and connect them in a downward progression, but also to begin with the last saying and link them in an ascending order.
2. What meanings might "cease to exist" have? It could possibly denote destruction, but it might also mean something else entirely.
3. The relationship of life and death is interesting in this collection of sayings. What is that relationship and how does one move from one state to the other?
4. Is there a connection between light and fire?
5. If one emerged back into the light, where would one be coming from?
6. The existence of the states of twoness and oneness are important themes not only in this logion but also in the rest of the Gospel. What does it mean to "realize your twoness?" Why would such a realization be important in the quest for wisdom?

Personal Reflections

also became two. *Both phrases suggest that something new is created out of something else.*

b. The second parallel construction has to do with "being" something. In this second grouping the phrase **emerge back into the light** *and* **come to realize your twoness again** *suggest that coming to dwell in the Light again will reveal twoness.*

LOGION 12

His students said,

We know we cannot
hold on to you,
so who will lead us then?

Yeshua said,

"Wherever it is that you find yourselves,
turn to James, one of the Just
for whom heaven and earth
have come into being."

Academic Translation

Yeshua's students said to him, "We know that you will slip from our grasp. Who, then, will be the great one over us?" Yeshua said, "When you get to that place, you will be going to James the Just, the one for whom heaven and earth came into being."

Notes

a. The phrase **we cannot hold on to you** (and in the Academic translation "you will slip from our grasp") is literally "leave our hand" in the Coptic version. In other translations this sentence is typically rendered, "We know that you will leave us. Who then will be our leader?" Our text seeks to preserve something of the original flavor and wording of the Coptic text in order to indicate other, more subtle meanings.

QUESTIONS FOR REFLECTION

1. This and the next saying center around two individuals both who were important in early Christianity as well as the mention of two other students and their responses. There may be a subtle link between this and the next saying to the collection of sayings in the previous logion. Explore that link. Perhaps there are even more than one.

2. From the previous list of sayings what could have sparked the question which the students raised? What are their fears and concerns? How does Yeshua answer those issues?

3. James (the Just), the leader of the first community of students in Jerusalem, was related to Jesus by birth as brother or half-brother. He was martyred early in the history of Christianity. How is the title, "Just One," an important historical clue?

4. If "turning to James" is only a future event in history, this saying has one meaning. If it is also an interior event in the personal development of his students, it may mean something else entirely. Imagine both, an exoteric interpretation as well as an esoteric (inner or spiritual) interpretation. What other aspects in this saying might support the esoteric interpretation?

Personal Reflections

b. The phrase **wherever it is that you find yourself** could also be translated, "When you get there…" The "place" Yeshua speaks of perhaps does not refer to topography at all, but to a moment in time, or more importantly, to a stage or state in their inner development.

c. **James, a Just One** could also be translated as "Jacob the Righteous," though the convention of James the Just is a traditional designation. However the term "Just" appears to translate a more historically significant word, "tzaddik" referring to a spiritual movement within post-Alexandrian Judaism that seems to be at the roots of the traditions of Merkava and Kabbalistic Judaism.

LOGION 13

Yeshua asked his students,

"Tell me, then, who am I like?
To whom will you
compare me?"

Simon Peter said,
"You are like a just angel."

Matthew said,
"You are a philosopher of wisdom."

Thomas said,
"Master, I cannot find words to express
who you really are."

Yeshua said,
"Thomas, it is no longer necessary
for me to be your Master
for you are drinking from the gushing
spring I have opened for you,
and you have become intoxicated."

Academic Translation

Yeshua said to his students, "Tell me, who am I like? To what can you compare me?" Simon Peter said, "You resemble a just angel." Matthew said, "You are like a wise philosopher." Thomas said to him, "Master, my mouth is unable to express who you resemble." Jesus said, "Because you have drunk from and are intoxicated by the flowing spring I have created for you, I am not your Master." Then withdrawing he took him aside and spoke three sayings to him. When Thomas returned to his companions they asked him, "What did Jesus say to you?" Thomas replied, "If I tell you even one of the sayings he

Then Yeshua took Thomas aside and spoke three sayings to him in private. When Thomas returned to the company of his companions they, of course, asked him, "What did Yeshua say to you?"

"If I were to tell you even one of the things he spoke to me," Thomas replied, "you would pick up these rocks and stone me, and then fire would blaze out of them and burn you."

spoke to me, you will pick up rocks and stone me, and fire will come out of the stones and burn you."

Notes

a. The term **just angel** *could also be translated as "righteous angel."*

b. Thomas' reply that he **cannot find words** *is literally in Coptic, "my mouth is unable to accept who you resemble." This indicates both inability to speak (and form the right words in speech), or to say out-loud what comes to mind.*

c. Translating the phrase **I am no longer your Master** *is strongly implied by Yeshua's statement indicating this is true "because...."*

d. The term **flowing spring** *could also be translated as "bubbling spring" though to bubble up means to flow, indicating "living water" in distinction to the still water of a cistern.*

e. The words **I have opened up for you** *(or in the Academic version,* "I have created for you") *translates the literal "I have measured" which seems not to have anything to do with measurement per se, but rather to create or open up.*

f. **Three sayings** *could just as easily be translated as "three words," but the indications are from what follows that these are* **logia**. *It makes sense to understand that Yeshua has continued the teaching in the form of sayings which are the basis of this entire text.*

QUESTIONS FOR REFLECTION

1. This is the first time that Yeshua questions his students. What seems to be the purpose of such an inquiry?
2. Compare the three answers the students give to Yeshua's question. Why does Thomas' answer appear to be the one Yeshua is looking for? What is different about it?
3. What might the link between James and Thomas be?
4. Thomas' inner state appears to be quite different from that of the other students. How can you tell that the inner state of the other students is unsuitable in some way whereas Thomas' is appropriate? What does it mean that Thomas has become intoxicated? What is the symbolism that is being used here, and how does it relate to Yeshua?
5. Once again fire is introduced in this saying. Is it different or the same fire from the other references?
6. We, of course, would like to be "let in on the secret" as well. What in fact did Yeshua say to Thomas? What was it about these sayings that would so disturb the other students that they might want to stone Thomas for repeating them?

Personal Reflections

LOGION 14

Yeshua says,

If you fast, you will only be giving
   birth to sin in yourself.
   If you pray,
your prayers will come back
to haunt you.
If you give to charity,
you will create evil
within your own spirit.

If, however, you travel through
a region and they welcome you,
eat whatever is put in front of you,
and heal their sick.
For it is not what goes into your mouth
that contaminates you,
but what comes out of it.

Academic Translation

Yeshua said this to them: "If you should fast you will give birth to sin in yourself. If you should pray your prayers will judge you. If you should give alms you will create evil in your spirit. If you should go to any land, walking in that region, and they receive you, eat whatever is put in front of you, and heal the sick among them. For it is not what goes into your mouth but what comes out of it which defiles you."

QUESTIONS FOR REFLECTION

1. It is interesting that the first three statements of this logion follow immediately from the conversation about Yeshua's three secret teachings to Thomas. Proximity and linkage suggest that these may indeed be the very statements that Yeshua made in private. If they are, why would they trouble the other students so badly?
2. Is Yeshua against fasting, prayer, and the giving of charity? Is that what this saying is trying to teach, or is it something else? What other possibilities are there?
3. How could it be that fasting would give birth to sin in an individual, or prayers return to haunt the individual who prays them, or that the giving of charity would create a form of inner evil?
4. How is the second part of this saying a commentary on the first?
5. How might the two parts of this saying illustrate two different inner states within Yeshua's own students?
6. Where will the journeying ultimately take the students of Yeshua? In what other regions might they be traveling? Where might they be going?

Personal Reflections

Notes

a. The idea of giving birth to sin is very strong in the opening line. It could even be more strongly taken to mean that you beget (or father) a child called "sin" in your very own being.

b. The Coptic text preserves the Greek word **judge** *here to specify an act of sentencing someone in a court of law. Some translations generalize the more literal* **create evil within your own spirit** *and say instead "do damage to yourself." It is certainly possible to translate it in this milder way, but the dynamic translation focuses upon the particular idea of the active creation of evil in the realm of one's own spirit.*

LOGION 15

Yeshua says,

When the time comes
and you are able to look
upon the Unborn One,
fall prostrate in worship,
for you have found your own true Father,
(your Source and Origin at last).

Academic Translation

Yeshua said, "When you come to look upon One not born of woman, fall on your face and worship, for that One is your Father."

QUESTIONS FOR REFLECTION

1. How might this saying be related to the experience and inner life of Yeshua himself?
2. What is the time Yeshua is talking about? When will it be and how does it create an ability to see?
3. Who is the Unborn One? Why is it important to look for or see this One?
4. How is it that this Unborn One is a father or parent? Is the intent of this saying upon male fathering or on something else entirely?

Personal Reflections

Notes

a. The literal rendering of the phrase **the Unborn One** *is "the One not born of woman." "The un-Begotten One" could also be easily substituted.*

b. The last phrase in italics is added to indicate one of the important meanings of the world **father**.

LOGION 16

Yeshua says,

Some of you are thinking
perhaps that I have come into
the cosmos to bring it peace.

No!
You do not yet realize
that I have come to throw it
into utter chaos
through burning, blade, and battle.

Five will be living in one household.
Three will face off against two,
and two against three.
Parents will rise up against children,
and children against their parents,
until at last they shall stand united
on their own feet.

Academic Translation

Yeshua said, "Some are thinking perhaps that I have come to cast peace into the cosmos. They do not yet realize that I have come to cast division upon the earth: fire, sword, war. Five will be in a house. Three will be against two, and two against three. The father against the son, and the son against the father, but they will stand as solitaries on their own feet."

Notes

a. The phrase **throw it into chaos** *is based upon the word "division" which can also be understood as separation and by extension disunity. Separation (to separate out) also expresses the idea of discrimination.*

b. The term **battle** *can be translated by the words: combat, war, and conflict.*

QUESTIONS FOR REFLECTION

1. This saying stands in stark contrast to the image we often have of Yeshua, as someone who is totally non-threatening and we need never be alarmed by him. But is this assessment correct? Perhaps we have been wrong about him for far too long.
2. To understand this logion we need to think carefully about what the cosmos actually is. In the writings of the early Christians it did not refer so much to the physical universe, but to the world of human invention. We might call it "the civilized world." Why might Yeshua want to throw that "cosmos" into chaos?
3. How is the ability to see mentioned in the last saying related to what Yeshua does in this one?
4. The three words **burning**, **blade**, and **battle**, could also be translated as fire, sword and war. How do these images relate to any previous saying?
5. What are the ultimate effects of Yeshua's act and the consequent chaos? What is Yeshua trying to accomplish in the end?
6. What does the act of uniting in order to stand on their own feet mean symbolically?
7. What might happen in this new united state?

Personal Reflections

c. The phrase **stand united** *is translated from a very particular Greek word* **monachos** *which means solitary, single, or alone. Later in Christian history this term is used for an ascetic or a monk. The word here translates a specfic Semitic idea, that of singleness (**ihidaya**) or its equivalent in other Semitic languages (Aramaic, Syriac, Hebrew, Arabic), referring to oneness. It signifies the reintegration and unification of parts into a single totality or whole. [See Bruno Barnhart's* **The Good Wine**, *NY: Paulist Press, 1993, 368-371].*

LOGION 17

Yeshua says,

What your own eyes cannot see,
your human ears
do not hear,
your physical hands cannot touch,
and what is inconceivable to the human
mind—that I will give to you!

Academic Translation

Yeshua said, "I will give you what no eye has seen, no ear has heard, what no hand has touched, and has never occurred to the human mind.

QUESTIONS FOR REFLECTION

1. Notice that words similar to this saying are found in St. Paul's first letter to the Corinthians (I Cor. 2:9). What might be the relationship between the meaning and contest of this saying and the reference in Paul's letter?

2. How is this gift of seeing, hearing, and touching what is inconceivable to the human mind, related to any of the sayings around it?

3. Ultimately, what is this gift?

Notes

a. Words very similar to this appear in St. Paul's first letter to the Corinthians (I Cor. 2: 9). The word **mind** *could also be translated as "heart."*

LOGION 18

His student said to him,

So, tell us, then,
   what our end and
   destiny will be?"

Yeshua answered,

"Have you already discovered
your origin so that now
you are free to seek after your end?
It is only at your source
that you will find your destiny.
Blessed are those who come to stand in
their place of origination,
for it is there that they will know their
end—never tasting death."

Academic Translation

The disciples said to him, "Speak to us about our end. How will it be?" Yeshua said, "Have you unveiled the Origin, so that now you are seeking after the end? It is at the place of origination that the end will also be. Blessed is the one whose feet will stand at the beginning, and know the end. That one will not taste death."

QUESTIONS FOR REFLECTION

1. What do you think has raised the students' question?
2. How does Yeshua answer their question?
3. This saying expresses something of the complexity of the wisdom teaching out of which Yeshua and Thomas speak. Notice that the place of standing, mentioned earlier, is at once the beginning and the end. If you were to diagram this idea, how would you do it?
4. Does this description remind you of any other phraseology in the canonical texts of Scriptures?
5. How could standing at the place of origination be the key to one's destiny?

Personal Reflections

Notes

a. The phrase **have you already discovered your origin** *is typically translated, "Have you discovered (or found) the beginning?" It translates the same Greek term* **arche** *which is also used in John 1. Though this way of translating the term has a long and venerable history, because of what follows in the next saying (Logion 19), and the fact that such a beginning may lie outside of time itself (and not simply at its temporal beginning), the word* **origin** *is used rather than a beginning point in time.*

LOGION 19

Yeshua says,

Blessed are all who come
        to live at the point of arising,
        their "genesis,"
before they came into temporality.

If you become my students,
listening deeply to my words,
even these stones will serve to you.

And in paradise
five evergreen trees await you.
They do not change in summer
nor shed their leaves in winter.
If you come to know them,
you will not know the taste of death.

Academic Translation

Yeshua said, "Blessed are those who come to exist at the beginning before they came into existence. If you should become my students, listening to my words, these stones will serve you. For you have there in paradise five trees that are unchanged in summer and do not lose their leaves in winter. The one who knows them will not taste death."

1. Notice how this and the previous logion are linked. Both express similar ideas and wording.

2. What new idea is added to the wisdom teaching concerning one's place of origin? Where is that place and, according to this idea, where do humans come from?

3. What does it mean to "live" in this place now?

4. What other references to stones have been expressed in Thomas' Gospel? How might these be linked?

5. What other word or idea is added to describe the place of arising?

6. What significance does the number five have in this saying? How could it be related to anything said previously in this text? What do trees in paradise signify?

Personal Reflections

Notes

a. The first line of this saying can be translated, "Blessed are those who come to be at the beginning before they come to be." The original word upon which **the point of arising (genesis)** is based is different from the one translated as **origin** (and **origination**) in the previous logion (based upon the Greek word *arche*).

b. The wording **If you become my students** in the original reads "If you should come to be to me a disciple." The word **serve** (the Greek word **diakonei**), means to minister and eventually expresses the diaconal ministry of the church.

LOGION 20

His students said to him,

"Tell us about this kingdom
of yours in the heavens.
What is it like?"

Yeshua answered them,

"Let me compare it to a mustard seed,
the smallest of all seeds.
When it falls into prepared ground,
it grows into a great tree capable of
sheltering the birds of the sky."

Academic Translation

His disciples said to Yeshua, "Tell us about this 'kingdom of the heavens.' To what is it comparable?" Yeshua answered them, "It can be compared to a mustard seed—the smallest of all seeds—but when it falls onto prepared ground, it sends out a great branch in which the birds of the sky can shelter."

QUESTIONS FOR REFLECTION

1. Once again, the way these sayings are juxtaposed suggests that something in the previous saying (or sayings) prompted the students' questions. What might those connections be?
2. This logion is another based upon agricultural metaphors. If you considered similar metaphors which came before it, how might the meaning of this and other sayings be related?
3. Notice that Yeshua uses the metaphors of the seed, a tree, and birds of the sky. If these symbolize spiritual realities, what do they denote?
4. What happens to prepared ground?

Personal Reflections

Notes

a. The word **heavens** *is literal, for it is in plural form in the original text. The word* **sky** *can also be translated "heaven."*

LOGION 21

Miriam said,

Then tell us, Master,
        what your students are like?
        How would you describe them?"

He answered,

"They are like small children
living in a field not their own.
When the landlords return and demand,
'Give us back our field!'
the children return it by
simply stripping themselves
and standing naked before them.

"So then, I must also tell you this:
If a householder knows for sure that
thieves are coming to steal his goods,
he will keep careful watch before they
get there to prevent them from tunneling
in and taking his possessions.
You, too, from your beginnings,
must keep a watchful eye on the cosmos,
binding great power to yourselves
so that thieves cannot find a way

to get to you.
Pay attention then.
Any outside help you look for
they will try to seize first.
May there be someone among you
who truly understands this.

"So listen carefully,
if you have an ear for this!
When the fruit was ripe,
ready to burst,
the harvester came quickly,
sickle in hand,
and took it."

Academic Translation

Marian asked Yeshua, "To what do you compare your students?" Yeshua replied, "They resemble small children living in a vast field which is not theirs. When the regents of that countryside returned they said, 'Give our field back to us!' So in order to return the field, the children stripped naked in their presence. I, therefore, also speak of it in this way: If the governor of a household realizes that a thief is coming, he will keep watch before he gets there to prevent him from tunneling into his domain and stealing his possessions. So from the beginning of the cosmos, therefore, you must also keep watch and bind great power to yourselves lest thieves find a way to get to you, because they will seize the external

Academic Translation

help you look for. Let there be a master of understanding among you. When the fruit was ripe he came quickly, sickle in hand, and harvested it. Whoever has ears for this let them listen."

Notes

a. The **landlords** *can also be thought of as "regents" signifying owners or lords of the land.*

b. **Field** *can also be translated as "countryside" which denotes wide agricultural lands.*

c. A **householder** *is also an "owner" or "governor" of a household.*

d. In the original text the place into which the thief tunnels is said to be a "kingdom" (or in the Academic version, a "domain").

e. **Binding great power to your-**

QUESTIONS FOR REFLECTION

1. Miriam, a female follower of Yeshua has a question of her own about his students, the ones who are listening and learning?
2. Yeshua's answer and description of his students is astonishing, for it seems so unlike anything we might have heard before. Does anything in that first description fit with other parts of Yeshua's teaching?
3. Many questions arise out of this complex logion. What is the field the students are living in? Who are its landlords? How does stripping and standing naked return possession of the field back to the landlords?
4. What might the metaphors of stripping and standing naked symbolize?
5. In the next part of the logion there is a contrasting idea, having to do with what the householder must do to prevent burglary. What are the contrasting verbs?
6. Are the thieves mentioned later the same as the landlords, or are they different?
7. What do these "cosmic thieves" try to do? What are the preventative actions necessary to keep the thieves at bay?
8. What is the significance of "outside help?"
9. The final action in this saying uses another agricultural metaphor, but at a different point in the cycle of farming.
10. What is the harvester looking for and how might that relate to the two previous parts of the logion?

Personal Reflections

self is idiomatically "to belt great power to one's loins."

f. The word **beginning** *used in this phrase is the same one used in Logion 19 indicating perhaps the temporal beginning point.*

g. The word **ripe** *translates the literal "split open."*

LOGION 22

Yeshua noticed infants nursing and said
to his students,

These little ones taking milk are
like those on their way into the
kingdom."

So they asked him,

"If we too are 'little ones'
are we on our way into the kingdom?"

Yeshua replied,

"When you are able
to make two become one,
the inside like the outside,
and the outside like the inside,
the higher like the lower,
so that a man is no longer male,
and a woman, female,
but male and female
become a single whole;
when you are able to fashion
an eye to replace an eye,

and form a hand in place of a hand,
or a foot for a foot,
making one image supercede another
—then you will enter in."

Academic Translation

Yeshua noticed children nursing and said to his students, "These little ones who are taking in milk are like those on their way into the kingdom." So they asked him, "If we are the 'little ones,' then are we also on our way into the kingdom?" Yeshua replied, "When you come to make the two into one, and if you make the inside like the outside and the outside like the inside, that which is above like that which is below, and male and female become a single whole—so that the male is no longer male or the female, female; when you fashion an eye in place of an eye, and form a hand to replace a hand, and one foot to replace another; when you make one image supersede another, then you will enter in."

QUESTIONS FOR REFLECTION

1. Like the last logion, this one too is full of strange and interesting metaphors. Here the teaching about movement toward the Kingdom and the doctrine of twoness and oneness is graphically expressed.
2. Yeshua's first statement concerning entry into the Kingdom is not unlike other sayings found in the canonical Gospels. What does the symbolism of nursing imply?
3. At the beginning of the sayings concerning oneness a number of crucial distinctions are made. If you were to diagram the relationships between what appear to be opposites, how would you do that?
4. What kind of androgyny is being encouraged in this saying?
5. If entering the Kingdom is dependent upon superimposition of images, what might this describe? How might that happen practically? What assistance might that require?

Personal Reflections

Notes

a. The terms **nursing** and **taking milk** are the same in the original text.

b. The term **image** is the Greek word **ikon** used later, of course, in Christian art.

c. The words **single whole** translates the same terms in Logion 4 and the saying which follows.

LOGION 23

Yeshua says,

I choose you,
  one from a thousand,
  two from ten-thousand,
and you will stand to your own feet
having become single and whole.

Academic Translation

Yeshua said, "I shall choose you, one from a thousand, two from ten thousand, and they will stand to their feet as a unity of one.

QUESTIONS FOR REFLECTION

1. Notice the two action verbs in this saying. What are they and how are they related?
2. If Yeshua is the chooser, what is his role after the choice is made?
3. What is the purpose of his choosing?
4. What are the ratios between the chosen and those outside the choice?
5. In what other sayings are the ideas of standing and wholeness and unity mentioned? What is the relationship between these two rather different terms?

Personal Reflections

Notes

a. The final phrase has been translated as **a single whole**. *It could also be understood as a "unitary being." This last phrase is also the same as the final wording of Logion 16 except for the last word,* **monachos** *which appears to mean the same thing.*

LOGION 24

His students said to him,

"Take us to the place where you are,
since we are required to seek
after it."

He answered them,

"Whoever has an ear for this
should listen carefully!
Light shines out from the center
of a being of light
and illuminates the whole cosmos.
Whoever fails to become light
is a source of darkness."

Academic Translation

His students said to him, "Show us the place where you are, since it is necessary that we seek for it." Yeshua replied, "Whoever has an ear for this should listen. Light exists on the inside of a being of light which becomes light for the whole cosmos. The one who fails to become light is darkness. "

QUESTIONS FOR REFLECTION

1. Is the "place" the students of Yeshua seek related to the previous saying? How?
2. Yeshua's answer redirects the students to such a "place." Where are the students to seek?
3. How would you define a "being of light?"
4. How would you contrast it to its opposite?
5. Light appears at the center of a person, but also in relationship to the cosmos. Relationship to the cosmos has been mentioned before, but through another metaphor (Logion 10). How might this saying be a commentary on other mentions of the cosmos?
6. Is the cosmos a place of light or of darkness? In either case, how is it so?

Notes

a. The term **place** *is the same word* **topos** *used in Logion 4.*

b. The **being of light** *translates the literal term "man of light."*

LOGION 25

Yeshua says,

Love your brother and your sister
as your very own being.
Protect them as you would the
pupil of your eye.

Academic Translation

Yeshua said, "Love your brother (and sister) as your own self. Protect them as you would the pupil of your eye."

QUESTIONS FOR REFLECTION

1. The use of the metaphor of light in the previous saying appears to be connected to this saying. How? Logia 24 and 25 also seem to relate to the next two sayings (L26 and L27). Examine all of them together to determine how they might be related.

2. How does one protect a brother or a sister? In what form does the protection come?

3. This particular saying relates to statements in the canonical Gospels as well as the Hebrew Scriptures. Do you recognize what those connections are?

Personal Reflections

Notes

a. The word **being** (or "self") could also be translated as "soul."

Logion 26

Yeshua says,

You detect a speck
in your brother's eye,
but fail to perceive the beam
sticking out of your own.
Remove the timber from your eye,
and you will see clearly enough
to extract the speck lodged
in the eye of your brother.

Academic Translation

Yeshua said, "You see the speck that in your brother's eye, but the beam in your own eye you do not see. When you are able to take the beam out of your own eye, you will see to remove the speck from your brother's eye."

QUESTIONS FOR REFLECTION

1. Attending to oneself and to others seems to be crucial to the care of the cosmos and to the wisdom of Logia 25 and 26. In each saying verbs are used in two sets of pairs. Notice their intrinsic relationship. How would you describe them?
2. How does discernment work according to this saying?
3. How do you extract the offending obstruction to sight?

Notes

a. The concept of seeing **clearly enough** *in the Coptic text has to do with the ability to see "outward" or "outside" as it is literally expressed.*

LOGION 27

Yeshua says,

If you do not fast from the cosmos,
    you will never grasp Reality.
    If you cannot find rest
on the day of rest,
you will never feast
your eyes on God.

Academic
Translation

Yeshua said, "If
you do not fast
from the cosmos
you will never find
the Kingdom. If
you do not make
the Sabbath,
Sabbath, you will
never see the
Father."

QUESTIONS FOR REFLECTION

1. Two very interesting statements about spiritual practice and its results are made in this logion. How are these spiritual practices and their effects described? Put them in your own words so you can better understand and explain them.
2. How might the two statements be related?
3. Notice that Yeshua gives positive valuation here to fasting in contrast to Logion 16. Why does he speak negatively in one and positively in the other? What is the difference between them?
4. How does one fast from the cosmos?
5. What does "resting on the day of rest" (the Sabbath) mean?

Personal Reflections

Notes

a. The word **grasp** *is the same Coptic word found in the opening logion.*

b. The word **rest** *translates the Hebrew word "Sabbath" which is the day of rest.*

c. The contrast to **fast,** *in the first line, is* feast *in the last line. This particular way of translating expresses the concept of seeing or looking upon God as the Father so that it "feeds" the soul.*

LOGION 28

Yeshua says,

I stood to my feet
in the midst of the cosmos,
appearing outwardly in flesh.
I discovered that all were drunk
and none were thirsty,
and my soul ached for
the children of humanity.
For their hearts are blind
and they cannot see from within.
They have come into the cosmos empty,
and they are leaving it empty.
At the moment you are inebriated,
but free from the effects of wine,
you too may turn and stand.

Academic Translation

Yeshua said, "I took my stand in the midst of the cosmos and I appeared outwardly to them in flesh. I discovered that all were drunk and no one was thirsting, and my soul ached for the sons (and daughters) of humanity, for their hearts are blinded and they can no longer see outwardly. They have come into the cosmos empty, and they are seeking to leave it empty. At present they are drunk, but when they rid themselves of their wine, then they too will turn inwardly (*metanoia*)."

Notes

a. Many of the words used in this logion are of particular significance. The first phrase is metaphorically important because it mirrors the last phrase. Literally the first phrase is "I stood to my feet" which is a symbolic

QUESTIONS FOR REFLECTION

1. Various statements are made about the cosmos in this and previous sayings (Logia 24, 27). Here Yeshua tells why he came into the cosmos and what he has discovered about it. What are his discoveries? How do they relate to the other statements about the cosmos made previously?
2. What does it mean for a person to be drunk in the cosmos?
3. Yeshua describes the current condition of humanity. What is his diagnosis?
4. This saying tells us many things about Yeshua, his experience and his mission. What are they?
5. Notice that the condition of inebriation has been used before (Logion 13). There is a definite contrast between them. What is the difference?
6. The image of standing is used again in this saying and the word for it in the original text is **metanoia**, which is often translated in English as "repent," but the word describes something more. What inner state is Yeshua hoping to see?

Personal Reflections

way of expressing the final Greek term metanoia used in the Coptic text and conventionally translated as "repent" or "repentance." Such a translation misses the import of the Greek term itself, having to do with reorienting one's nous or conscious awareness. This phraseology is, of course, used many times in the canonical Gospels and translated so as to miss the implication of Thomas' metaphor. Yeshua stands up, out of the cosmos and aligns himself vertically. All the rest of humanity is in the state or position of horizontal sleep (or inner spiritual blindness) from the satiating effects of wine from the cosmos.

b. All this Yeshua discovers (the same word which has been used in the first and other sayings) when he is enfleshed in the cosmos (the term used to express the theological concept of incarnation).

LOGION 29

Yeshua says,

If flesh came into existence
   for the sake of spirit,
   it is a wonder,
but if spirit exists for the sake of flesh,
it is a wonder of wonders.
I am truly astonished
at how such richness
came to dwell in such poverty.

Academic Translation

Yeshua said, "If the flesh came into being because of spirit, it is a wonder. If the spirit exists because of the body it is a wonder of wonders. But I am made to wonder how such richness came to be placed in such poverty."

QUESTIONS FOR REFLECTION

1. This saying continues to explain the work of Yeshua, using new and surprising contrasts. Often flesh and spirit are split apart. How are they related (or even united) in this logion?
2. This saying appears to pinpoint one of the wonders mentioned in the second logion. How might Yeshua's statement clear up the confusion?
3. In the previous saying, freedom is contrasted with emptiness (and yet being full of wine). In this saying poverty is contrasted with richness. Are these inner states related? How? In combination, what fuller wisdom does this teach?

Personal Reflections

Notes

a. The word **flesh** has significance in the whole of the Christian tradition. St. Paul uses it as a kind of code word for a human being's relationship to the body; one in which there is dependency and even addiction. In the Gospel of Thomas it appears to have that same connotation (see Logion 112), but here it may simply refer to materiality or the physical form of humanity. Both "flesh" and "the body" are used in the original text as indicated above. In each case spirit and matter (flesh or body) appear to have an intimate and positive relationship.

b. The word **wonder** is the same as used in Logion 2.

LOGION 30

Yeshua says,

Where there are
three divinities,
God is present.
Where one or two exist,
I am there.

Academic Translation

Yeshua said, "In the place where there are three gods, they are divine (or where there are three divinities, God is present). In that place where there are two or one, I am there."

QUESTIONS FOR REFLECTION

1. This saying which could be translated a number of different ways seems strange and perplexing. Whatever the correct translation may be, the focus of it appears to be a form of subtraction or reduction. How might that be explained?
2. How would this emphasis relate to what has just been said in the previous saying?
3. What is the significance of the words "I Am?" How might the last phrase of the saying be rewritten to emphasize this idea?
4. When the I Am is present what does it seek to do?

Personal Reflections

Notes

a. This is one of the most perplexing of the Logia. A study of the surviving Greek version (Oxyrynchus Papyrii 1, lines 23-27) under ultraviolet light has led Harold W. Attridge to conclude that the Coptic text is inaccurate. His restoration of the text is used as a basis for the dynamic translation. Iterations of the Coptic version are used immediately above. This information was noted by Peter Kirby in an Internet discussion group on the Gospel of Thomas, June 24, 2002.

LOGION 31

Yeshua says,

No prophet is
welcomed home.
        No healer cures acquaintances.

Academic Translation

Yeshua said, "No prophet is welcomed in his own village. No physician heals those who know him."

QUESTIONS FOR REFLECTION

1. If Yeshua appears in the cosmos in spirit, what does he come to do? What are his functions?
2. The modern saying, "Familiarity breeds contempt" may apply to this logion. How?
3. What might a healer and a prophet come to do?

Personal Reflections

LOGION 32

Yeshua says,

A city built and fortified
on a mountain top cannot fall,
but neither can it be hidden.

Academic Translation

Yeshua said, "A city built and fortified on a high mountain cannot fall. Neither can it be hidden."

QUESTIONS FOR REFLECTION

1. What (or who) is this city? Where is the mountain top?
2. If something (a city or a person) is no longer hidden, what might its purpose be?

Personal Reflections

Notes

a. Two sets of actions apply to the city on a mountain top, building and fortifying. What is not completely clear from the text is whether fall (the same word as "discover" or "seize" used in the first logion) means fall down or be captured. Probably the latter.

LOGION 33

Yeshua says,

What you hear with one ear,
listen to with both,
and then proclaim
from the roof tops.
For no one lights a lamp
and then hides it away.
It is placed on a lamp-stand instead
where those who pass by
may see by its light.

Academic Translation

Yeshua said, "What you hear in one ear, listen to with your other ear and proclaim from the rooftops. No one lights a lamp and then places it in hiding. Instead a lamp is placed on a lamp stand where those who go in and out may see its light."

QUESTIONS FOR REFLECTION

1. Revelation and proclamation are the purpose of this logion. What sensory faculties are involved in this disclosure?
2. What are the purposes of voice and light?
3. Notice who the light affects. For whom will it be important?

Personal Reflections

Notes

a. The reference to the two ears is literally translated above, but appears to mean something closer to the way we would express it in the dynamic translation.

b. A scribal error may have changed the original wording from "hides it under a basket" to the Coptic **hides it away** *or places it in hiding.*

c. A more modern English idiom is also used in the final phrase.

LOGION 34

Yeshua says,

If the blind are leading the blind
they will topple together
into a pit.

**Academic
Translation**

Yeshua said, "If a
blind person leads
another who is
also blind, both
shall fall into a
pit."

QUESTIONS FOR REFLECTION

1. Comments about the absurdity of a
   "blind guide" are current in our culture as
   well. The reason is succinctly stated in
   this logion.
2. Who are the blind? What is the pit?
3. How do you overcome blindness?

Personal Reflections

LOGION 35

Yeshua says,

Y ou cannot take
a strong man's house by force
unless first you bind
his hands and remove him.

Academic Translation

Yeshua said, "There is no way that you can enter a strong man's house and take him by force unless you bind his hands. Only then can he be removed from the house."

QUESTIONS FOR REFLECTION

1. The notion of something being taken by force have been expressed in Logion 21. There the effects are different from what is described here, or are they?

2. What is the purpose of binding the strong man's hands? Who is he and what or where is his house?

3. Who might be doing this kind of forceful work?

Personal Reflections

Notes

a. It is interesting that the same locus of action and the same accomplishment are mentioned in a future saying (Logion 48). There, a house is also mentioned along with the action of "moving" or "removing." In this logion the emphasis appears to be on the emptying and clearing out of the house.

LOGION 36

Yeshua says,

Do not spend your time
from one day to the next
worrying about your
outer appearance, what you wear and
what you look like.

Academic Translation

Yeshua said, "Do not be anxious from morning to evening or from evening to morning about what you will put on."

QUESTIONS FOR REFLECTION

1. The emphasis in this saying is upon human activities which, in the end, amount to nothing. They are a waste of time. How important is this particular activity in human society? How much time would you imagine we spend thinking or worrying about what we wear or how we look?
2. What might be a better use of our time?
3. Are any of the previous sayings related to this one? How?
4. If Yeshua makes such a statement, his students must be concerned with outer appearance. What might they be worried about?

Personal Reflections

Notes

a. The lines **worrying about your outer appearance, what you wear and what you look like** *are extended in this way to put emphasis on the exterior focus which is the subject of this saying.*

LOGION 37

His students asked him,

When will you manifest
your self to us?
How long will it be
before we see you as you truly are?

Yeshua replied,

"On the day you strip yourselves naked
like those little children,
and take your clothes
and trample them on the ground under
your feet without shame,
then you will be able to look upon
the son of the Living One
without fear."

Academic Translation

His students asked him this, "On what day will you manifest yourself to us? On what day will be able to look upon you?" Yeshua said, "When you strip yourselves naked without being ashamed and take your garments and put them on the ground under your feet like those small children and trample them, then you will look upon the son of the Living One and not be afraid."

QUESTIONS FOR REFLECTION

1. Yeshua's students seem to have a problem in discerning Yeshua. What conclusions might we reach about them from this sort of trouble?
2. What is Yeshua "as he truly is?" What does this mean?
3. Yeshua's answer is startling, and refers back to a previous saying (Logion 21).
4. Interestingly in this and the previous saying clothes are mentioned. How might these be related to one another?
5. In making his statement about seeing, Yeshua names two inner conditions that appear to be true of his students. What are they and what is the optimal condition which Yeshua believes is necessary for seeing?
6. Yeshua names himself. What name does he use?
7. What sort of stripping away might this saying imply both now and in the future?

Personal Reflections

Notes

a. It is quite clear that in answering the questions raised by his students, Yeshua is referring back to Logion 21. This fact makes it certain that at least some of the sayings in the Gospel of Thomas are self-referential.

b. The term **son of the Living One** *is literally "the son of he who lives."*

LOGION 38

Yeshua says,

On many occasions
you have longed
to hear such words as
the ones that I am speaking to you,
but you had no one to go to.
The day will come again
when you will seek for me,
but will not be able to find me.

Academic Translation

Yeshua said, "Many times you have longed to listen to the words I am speaking to you, but you have had no one from whom you could hear them. There will be days when you will seek for me, but will not be able to find me."

QUESTIONS FOR REFLECTION

1. This saying speaks about personal loss and the future. It speaks about human longing and the inability to fulfill it. How had they experienced loss before?
2. For the followers of Yeshua why might this loss be the case in the future?

Personal Reflections

Notes

a. The term **words** *could also be "sayings" (or the parables of Yeshua).*

b. The word **find** *is the word for "discover or seize" used in the opening Logion.*

LOGION 39

Yeshua says,

Your scholars and religious leaders
    have taken the keys
    of knowledge and
locked them away.
They have not used them
to enter in, nor have they allowed those
desiring it to do so.
You, therefore, must be
as subtle as serpents and
as guileless as doves.

Academic Translation

Yeshua said, "The scribes and Pharisees took and hid the keys of knowledge. They did not go in, nor did they permit those who desired it to do so. You, however, are to be cunning like the serpents and innocent like the doves."

QUESTIONS FOR REFLECTION

1. If the previous saying relates to personal loss in the future, this logion has to do with religious loss. How can religion become a deficit, or false to itself?
2. If such a loss occurs in religious life, what is the student supposed to do?
3. How is a serpent subtle? How is a dove guileless (or innocent)?
4. How might one develop spiritual subtlety and innocence? What do these mean in practice?
5. How does the state of loss develop in religious life?

Personal Reflections

Notes

a. The term **keys of knowledge** *is literally "the keys of gnosis." The significance of this term suggests a form of knowing that is available in the realm of religion, but in our world often hidden or locked away.*

b. The words **serpents** *and* **doves** *have resonance with stories in the Genesis of the Torah.*

LOGION 40

Yeshua says,

A grapevine was planted
away from its Source
where it remains unprotected.
It will be torn out by its roots
and destroyed.

Academic Translation

Yeshua said, "They have planted a grapevine outside the Father and have not protected it. It will be pulled up by its roots and destroyed."

QUESTIONS FOR REFLECTION

1. In a number of the previous logia the implication is that there is need for some kind of decisive (or perhaps violent) action. When or why might that be necessary? Can you think of an instance where you felt the need for violent action?
2. How would you describe a grapevine "planted outside its Source?"
3. Who, do you think, did the planting? Who will do the uprooting?
4. Why would such violence be enacted, at least on a spiritual level? What might that be like?

Personal Reflections

Notes

a. This logion is an example of a particular feature of the Coptic language where there is no formal passive voice. However, as Michael Grondin has expressed it, "…the passive voice being assumed if the word 'they' lacks a referent" [See Michael Grondin's important website]. In the dynamic version the passive voice is used. In the academic version the active voice is maintained which may, in fact, refer to the scribes and Pharisees of the previous logion.

b. The word **Source** is literally in the Coptic text "Father" which can, in first-century understanding, refer to God as Source.

c. The word **unprotected** is the same one for **fortified** in Logion 32.

LOGION 41

Yeshua says,

To the one who has
something in hand,
more will be given.
To the one whose hands hold nothing,
even that "nothing" will be taken away.

Academic Translation

Yeshua said, "To the one who has something in hand, more will be given. To the one who is empty handed even that little bit will be taken away."

QUESTIONS FOR REFLECTION

1. The metaphor of the hand (or hands) is used in this Gospel as well as in the canonical Gospels. How might they be related?
2. Both absence (or loss) and possession are the subject of this saying. What possession might be of value and kept?
3. What "nothing" might need to be taken away?

Personal Reflections

Notes

a. The term **nothing** is literally "that little bit."

LOGION 42

Yeshua says,

Come into being
as you pass
away.

Academic Translation

Yeshua said, "Come to be as you pass away."

QUESTIONS FOR REFLECTION

1. In this shortest of the sayings there appears to be a paradox. At the very moment of subtraction there is addition. What is being subtracted?
2. What is being added?
3. Why might this saying cause confusion or misunderstanding?
4. How might this give way to wonder?

Personal Reflections

Notes

a. This interesting phraseology has also been translated as "Become passers-by." It could also perhaps be translated, "Become yourself as you are passing away."

LOGION 43

His students said to him,

Who are you to
be saying
such things to us?"

Yeshua replied,

"Do you not realize who I am
from everything I have said to you?
Have you come to be like the Judeans
who either accept the tree,
but reject its fruit, or welcome the fruit
and despise the tree?"

Academic Translation

His students said, "Who are you to speak these things to us?" Yeshua replied, "Do you not realize who I am from what I have said to you? You have become instead like the Judeans who love the tree and hate its fruit, or love the fruit and hate the tree."

QUESTIONS FOR REFLECTION

1. Why might the students of Yeshua be offended at the previous saying, or question his authority as the source of it?
2. Yeshua's reply uses an agricultural metaphor contrasting two elements in a tree, root and fruit. What are these metaphors about?
3. Why might the difference between acceptance and rejection pose a spiritual difficulty?

Personal Reflections

Notes

a. The terms **reject** *and* **despise** *can also be translated "hate."* **Accept** *and* **welcome** *is conventionally translated with the term "love," as was done in the academic version above. It makes idiomatic sense, however, to use the more modern phraseology which helps us to better understand other logia as well.*

LOGION 44

Yeshua says,

You may speak against the Father
and it will be forgotten.
You may speak against the son
and it will be dropped.
But if you speak opposing
the sacred Spirit,
that is irrevocable
both in heaven and on earth.

Academic Translation

Yeshua said, "Whoever speaks out against the Father, it will be removed. Whoever speaks against the son, that too shall be dropped. But whoever speaks against the Spirit which is holy, shall not be removed either here on earth or in the heavens."

QUESTIONS FOR REFLECTION

1. Here, as in the canonical Gospels, Yeshua makes a distinction between opposition to Father or son in contrast to Spirit. What might be the crucial distinction between these?
2. Why would speaking in opposition to (or working against) Spirit be irrevocable?
3. How is this saying related to the previous logion as well as to the one which follows?

Personal Reflections

Notes

a. The Coptic text presents some interesting variations to the traditional phraseology we are used to in the canonical Gospels. First, Thomas uses the name "Father" in addition to the Son and the Spirit.

b. The traditional term of "blasphemy" is literally "to speak a word against" (also used in some of the canonical Gospels), and the traditional "forgive" is to "remove" or "take away."

LOGION 45

Yeshua says,

Grapes are not
harvested from thorns,
nor are figs gathered from
thistles — neither produce fruit.

Good people
bring goodness out of
a storehouse of inner treasure,
while evil ones bring wickedness
out of the repository of evil
collected in the heart.
It is from there that they speak.
For from the heart's overflow
evil enters the world.

Academic Translation

Yeshua said, "They do not harvest grapes from thorns, nor gather figs from thistles, neither of these bear fruit. A good man brings good out of his treasure. An evil man brings evil things out of the wickedness treasured in his heart – speaking evil. For out of the overflow of the heart he brings forth evil."

QUESTIONS FOR REFLECTION

1. Through another set of agricultural metaphors, Yeshua comments on the issue of speaking, raised in the previous logion. Grapes and thistles illustrate the issue in a way that is similar to root and fruit in Logion 42. How are these metaphors related?
2. Where is the treasure found?
3. There is a continuity of ideas between this and Logion 14. Are these Logia related in some way?
4. If the issue of goodness and wickedness is an inner condition, what determines that condition?

Personal Reflections

Notes

a. The word **heart** *can be translated with the word "mind," though something more than mental activity or the thinking capacity seems to be intended.*

LOGION 46

Yeshua says,

Among those born on earth
beginning from Adam to
John the Baptist,
no one has reached a higher state
than John — and you should
bow in honor before him.

Yet, I tell you this,
whoever of you becomes "a little child"
will not only know the kingdom,
but will be raised to a state
higher than John's.

Academic Translation

Yeshua said, "Among those born of woman from Adam to John the Baptist no one has been raised higher than John, so you should avert your eyes. However, I say this to you, whoever among you becomes "a little one" will know the kingdom and be raised higher than John."

QUESTIONS FOR REFLECTION

1. John the Baptist played an important initiatory role in the life of Yeshua. His teaching, perhaps, also had an immense impact on Yeshua, so he is being honored as the Teacher who has reached an advanced state. But there is one higher, that of the child? This, of course, appears to be another paradox. How can it be true?
2. The image of the child has been used a number of times before. Who is this little child, and what does it mean to become the child?
3. What state is opposite to that of the child?
4. What is the inner state of the child? How does one achieve it?
5. Why is it a higher state than John's?

Personal Reflections

Notes

a. The phrase **bow in honor before him** *is an idiomatic expression for the literal "avert your eyes." In many cultures, people who occupy a lower social rank keep their eyes averted when in the presence of a person of higher rank or order. Each way of translating this phrase indicates that one is to honor the higher station of John.*

LOGION 47

Yeshua says,

No one can mount two horses,
or draw two bows at once,
and you cannot serve
two masters at the same time.
If you honor one,
the other will be offended.

No one drinks a vintage wine
and immediately wants
to taste wine freshly bottled.
New wine is not put into
old containers lest it be ruined,
nor is aged wine put into
new barrels lest it spoil.

Also, old cloth is not sewn
onto new garments because
it only makes the tear worse.

Academic Translation

Yeshua said, "There is no way that a man can climb on the backs of two horses or draw two bows. A servant cannot serve two masters, lest he honor the one and the other despise him. No one drinks aged wine and immediately wants new wine to drink, and new wine is not poured into old skis lest they split open. Aged wine is not poured into fresh skins lest is be spoiled. Old patches are not sewn onto new cloth lest it be torn."

QUESTIONS FOR REFLECTION

1. Multiple images are juxtaposed to illustrate a number of important points. The images are put together in related sets. What are the images and what is their relationship?
2. The first set of metaphors uses numeration to illustrate a spiritual principle. What is the principle and how has it been used elsewhere in the text?
3. The second set speaks about various aspects of wine and their effects. How are these related to one another and to the final set of images?
4. To meet the conditions of each of these sets what would need to be done? What kind of being would be created as a result? What would be the end result of such activity?

Notes

a. The entire text of the dynamic version is given full, modern idiomatic expression. The particular difference is between the ancient and the modern containers for wine.

Logion 48

Yeshua says,

Should two make peace
    in one house,
        they could speak the word,
"Move!" to a mountain,
and it would obey them.

Academic Translation

Yeshua said, "Should two make peace together in a single house, they shall speak to the mountain and say, 'Move away!' and it will move."

Questions for Reflection

1. This is a very powerful image. Who are the two in one house? What is the house?
2. What does the making of peace entail?
3. Does the image of the mountain signify anything in particular?

Personal Reflections

Notes

a. The term **one house** *is more precisely the "single" state that has been mentioned in Logia 4, 22, and 23.*

LOGION 49

Yeshua says,

Blessed are those
chosen and unified.
The Realm of
the Kingdom is theirs.
For out of her you have come,
and back to her you are returning.

Academic Translation

Yeshua said, "Blessed are the solitary and chosen. For you will seize upon the Kingdom, because out of her you have come and to her you will return."

QUESTIONS FOR REFLECTION

1. Many themes expressed in this Gospel are summarized and clarified in this short saying. Why is the Realm of the Kingdom the possession of a unified being?
2. What does unification mean or entail?
3. Draw a diagram which illustrates the last sentence of the saying. How might it relate to the next logion?

Personal Reflections

Notes

a. The term **unified** *(or "solitary") is the special term which has been used in Logion 16 and later in Logion 75 which is the basis for English words monastic and monk. The force of it is perhaps best captured by the word* **unified** *since it refers to one who has reached a state of unification as Logion 16 suggests.*

b. The academic version preserves the important Coptic term "seizing hold of" the Kingdom used in the first Logion.

LOGION 50

Yeshua says,

Suppose you are asked,
  "Where have you come from?"
  say, "We have come from
the Light at its source,
from the place where it came forth and
was manifest as Image and Icon.

If you are asked,
"Are you that Light?"
say, "We are its children,
and chosen by the Source,
the Living Father."

If you are questioned,
"But what is the sign of
the Source within you?"
say, "It is movement and it is rest."

Academic Translation

Yeshua said, "If they say to you, 'Where have you come from?' Say, 'We have come out of the light, from where light came to be, and from that place which, on its own accord, it stood to its feet and appeared in their image.' If they should ask you, 'Are you he?' Say, 'We are his sons, and the chosen of the Living Father.' If they should ask you, 'What is the sign within yourself of your Father?' Say to them this, 'It is movement and it is rest.'"

QUESTIONS FOR REFLECTION

1. Three sets of questions are asked. Where might such questions be asked, and why might answers such as these be needed?
2. Yeshua's instructions about how to answer are interesting. What do they tell us? What kind of a cosmology is being described? Who are human beings in that kind of a cosmos?
3. What is the first manifestation of a human being?
4. Who is the Source and what is it like?
5. Movement and rest are opposites? How do they exist together, and how could they be the sign of the Source?

Personal Reflections

Notes

a. In whatever way this logion is translated it is difficult to fully express its complexity. The term **Light** *seems to be personified, since it literally "stands to its feet" manifesting as* **"Image and Icon,"** **ikon** *being the literal word. The action of "standing to its feet" has already been expressed in Logion 28, where the referent is clearly Yeshua himself. Much of this imagery is also articulated in the first chapter of St. John's Gospel concerning the* **Logos**.

b. The term **rest (anapausis)** *is significant since it is used in the Letter to the Hebrews as well as in the Greek version of Logion 2, and also later in Logia 51, 60, and 90.*

Logion 51

His students asked him,

When does 'rest' for the dead begin, and when will the new cosmos arrive?

Yeshua replied,

"What you are looking for is already here. You simply have not recognized it."

Academic Translation

His students said to him, "On what day will there be rest for the dead, and when is the new world coming?" Yeshua said, "That which you are looking for outwardly has already come, but you, you do not know it."

QUESTIONS FOR REFLECTION

1. The students' question is related to the previous logion. Have they understood the term **rest** and used it in the same way as Yeshua?
2. The students' question and Yeshua's answer is expressed in the context of time. How do their questions and Yeshua's answer related to time?
3. Why cannot (or do not) the students of Yeshua recognize the new cosmos?

Personal Reflections

Notes

a. The word **rest** is often translated as "repose," however, this obscures the fact that the same word used in the previous saying is in play here.

b. The conventional translation world has been replaced with the literal word **cosmos** in the dynamic version.

LOGION 52

His students said,

Each of Israel's twenty-four prophets spoke about you."

Yeshua said,

"You ignore the one living in your presence and talk only about the dead."

Academic Translation

His students said to him, "Twenty-four prophets spoke in Israel, and each of them have spoken through you." Yeshua said, "You have abandoned the living one in your presence and speak about the dead."

QUESTIONS FOR REFLECTION

1. Like the previous exchange, this one between Yeshua and his students, is also related to time. What is their concern and its relationship to time?
2. Does Yeshua agree with their statement about the twenty-four prophets?
3. Who is ignoring who in this exchange?
4. "One in the presence" has been mentioned before (Logion 5). How is this idea further qualified in this saying?

Personal Reflections

Notes

a. The students express their understanding of the prophets' relationship to Yeshua using the word **about**. The phrase is literally "down in you." This phraseology could also be rendered "through you" expressed in the academic version.

b. The phrase **the one living in your presence** is a literal rendering of the Coptic text.

LOGION 53

His students asked,

I s circumcision of
    any help to us?"

Yeshua replied,

"If it were your fathers would have
been born fully circumcised
from their mother's womb.
The only circumcision that will benefit
you at all is spiritual."

Academic Translation

His students asked him, "Is circumcision of any benefit to us or not?" Yeshua answered them, "If it were of benefit your fathers would have birthed you already circumcised out of your mother. The only true circumcision which will benefit you is in spirit."

QUESTIONS FOR REFLECTION

1. Besides the specific question about circumcision, what are the students of Yeshua's general concern in this and the last saying? Upon what are they focused?
2. Circumcision is the sign of the removal of flesh. How is that a spiritual issue beyond the cultural and religious duties of a Jew?
3. How would you describe spiritual circumcision?

Personal Reflections

Notes

a. The dynamic version takes some license in translating the issue of fathers being birthed (or as the literal text suggests "birthing" or "begetting") from their mothers.

b. Yeshua's final statement concerning spiritual circumcision is consonant with the entire Gospel tradition.

LOGION 54

Yeshua says,

You poor are blessed,
    for the realm of heaven
    is already yours.

Academic Translation

Yeshua said, "The blessed ones are the poor, for yours is the kingdom of the heavens."

QUESTIONS FOR REFLECTION

1. What is poverty? What does it mean to be poor?
2. Why does the realm of heaven (the Kingdom) already belong to the "poor?"
3. Where in time does this saying place the poor?
4. What other ways of being poor are there besides not having money or riches?

Personal Reflections

Notes

a. The term **poor** *is the same word used for* **poverty** *in Logion 3.*

b. The heavens *is literally a plural form.*

LOGION 55

Yeshua says,

Whoever does not
refuse father and mother
cannot become my student.
Whoever does not reject
brother and sister,
accepting the cross as I do,
is not ready for me.

Academic Translation

Yeshua said, "Whoever does not hate father and mother cannot become my student, and whoever does not hate brother or sister and carry the cross as I do does not deserve me."

QUESTIONS FOR REFLECTION

1. Who are the kinfolk of this saying? Should these be taken literally or figuratively?
2. What is this act of refusal and rejection? What forms do these take?
3. Why would such action make one ready for Yeshua?
4. What does readiness mean?

Personal Reflections

Notes

a. **Refuse** and **reject** express the word conventionally translated as "hate." It is clear from other sayings that hate has other meanings related to rejection and refusal (see Logion 43).

b. The last phrase could be translated as it has been in the academic version, "deserve me" (suggested by the word's use in Logion 85).

LOGION 56

Yeshua says,

Those who make knowledge
of the cosmos their specialty
have made friends with a corpse,
but the cosmos is not worthy
of whose who know it to be so.

Academic Translation

Yeshua said, "Whoever has come to know the cosmos has grasped a corpse, but the cosmos is not worthy of whoever has "grasped" it as a corpse."

QUESTIONS FOR REFLECTION

1. This saying is focused upon two forms of knowledge. Each one concerns a particular topic. How would you describe this knowledge and its content?
2. Why is this special knowledge described as "friendship with a corpse?" How might this be so?
3. According to this saying, the final form of knowing elevates the worth of the person who possesses it. Why would this be true?
4. How might an individual gain this higher form of knowledge?

Personal Reflections

Notes

a. The word "cadaver" could easily replace the word **corpse**.

b. The phrase **made friends with** translates the familiar word "seize" as used in this, the first, and other sayings.

LOGION 57

Yeshua says,

God's realm is like this:
    A farmer planted good
    seed in his field,
but at night enemies came
and sowed it with weeds.
When he found out
he did not allow them to be
pulled up, saying,
"No, you might uproot the grain
along with the weeds. Wait till harvest.
It will be perfectly apparent then
which ones are the weeds,
and you may pull them out easily
and burn them."

Academic Translation

Yeshua said, "The kingdom of the Father is like a man who had good seed, but during the night his enemy came and sowed weeds among the good seed. The man, however, did not permit them to pull up the weeds saying, 'So you won't go and pull up the grain along with the weeds. On the day of harvest the weeds will be obvious and they can be pulled up and burned."

QUESTIONS FOR REFLECTION

1. Logion 57 continues the agricultural metaphors focusing upon processes and outcomes. The scenes depicted in this saying may be directly related to the ones in Logion 9, but here a complication is introduced. What do the weeds and the field symbolically represent?
2. What wisdom is this saying teaching?
3. What does waiting require?
4. What form of knowledge and experience is produced by the action required in this saying?

Personal Reflections

Notes

a. The dynamic translation has been made fully idiomatic.

LOGION 58

Yeshua says,

B lessed are the troubled ones.
They have seized
hold of life.

Academic Translation

Yeshua said, "Blessed is the one who is troubled, that one has found life."

QUESTIONS FOR REFLECTION

1. In the previous two sayings there is evidence of "signs of trouble." What might they be, and how could they be understood ultimately as a blessing and not a curse?
2. What form of troubling at work in this saying not only produces blessing, but also causes a human being to seize hold of life? What do you imagine is the relationship of these three ideas, troubling, blessing, and seizing hold of life?
3. The opposite of life is what? How does one "seize hold of life?"

Personal Reflections

Notes

a. The word **troubled** in this short saying could be translated in various ways; bothered, concerned, or distressed are also possible. This is an individual for whom life is not easy, and as a consequence has suffered. Nevertheless, the troubled person has **seized hold of life** in exactly the way that this word is used from the first saying onward.

LOGION 59

Yeshua says,

Give attention to
the Living Presence
while you are alive
so that when you die and have
the desire to do so,
you may have the power to attend.

Academic Translation

Yeshua said, "Pay attention to the one who lives while you are living, lest when you die and seek to see him you cannot find the power to do so."

QUESTIONS FOR REFLECTION

1. As wisdom teaching, what form of awareness is being encouraged in this saying? What power does this saying instruct us to seek?
2. What is its opposite power?
3. How will this form of awareness be used in the future of a human being?
4. This saying is related in subject matter to Logia 5 and 91. Compare these. What is the central teaching in each of these logia?
5. In this, the previous, and the following saying he subject of life and death is the focus. How would you connect them?

Personal Reflections

Notes

a. The translation of the literal "one who lives" is given as **Living Presence** *based on previous logion (particularly Logion 5 and 52).*

b. **Give attention** *translates the literal word "look" or "watch for."*

*c. The final phrase in the academic translation (***find the power to do so***) literally translates the text.*

LOGION 60

They saw a Samaritan
on his way to Judea
carrying a lamb.

Yeshua said, "Notice the Samaritan
with the lamb."

His disciples said, "He must be carrying it
in order to kill and eat it."

Yeshua responded, "As long as it is alive
he cannot eat it. Only after he has killed
it and it is dead will it be eaten."

They replied, "What other way is there?"

Yeshua said, "You must be careful
to find a place for yourselves
in the realm of eternal rest,
lest you too be killed and eaten."

1. This logion consists of a narrative in which
   dialogue and image are related to each

Academic Translation

Seeing a Samaritan taking a lamb into Judea, Yeshua said to his students, "Notice the one carrying the lamb." He students said, "He carries it so that he might kill and eat it." Yeshua replied, "While it is alive he will not eat it, only when he has killed it and it becomes a corpse will he do so." They said, "He cannot do it any other way." Yeshua said, "You also must seek for yourselves a place within the rest, so that you too do not become a corpse and they eat you."

QUESTIONS FOR REFLECTION

other in interesting and complex ways. What is the obvious subject matter in the dialogue? What is the historical context for understanding what is happening and what Yeshua and his students are observing?

2. What point is Yeshua trying to make using the actions of the Samaritan?
3. There appears to be a direct relationship to the subject matter of the previous saying. How are they related?
4. What is the relationship of this logion to time? Is it about the future? How are you the listener being oriented towards time?
5. What is the "eternal rest?" Is it now or in the future?
6. Based on this dialogue, in what ways can life and death to be described?
7. At death what must we possess? Do we need the same in life, or is there another need?

Personal Reflections

Notes

*a. The dynamic version has turned this **conversation** between Yeshua and his students into idiomatic English. The emphasis in the original text seems to be focused upon the corpse of the lamb after it has been killed.*

*b. The phraseology of **in the realm of eternal rest** translates the literal "place (**topos**) to you in rest."*

LOGION 61

Yeshua says,

Two will be resting on a bed.
One will die,
the other will live.

Salome said,
"Then how is it, Sir, that you,
coming from the one Source,
have rested on my coach
and eaten at my table?"

Yeshua said to her,
"I am he who has appeared to you
out of the Realm of Unity,
having been granted that which belongs
to my Father, its Source."

"I will be your student!" she exclaimed.

"Then I say this to you,
if you become whole
you will be full of Light.
If you remain fragmented
darkness will fill you."

Academic Translation

Yeshua said, "Two will rest on a couch. One will die. One will live." Salome said, "Who are you, sir, while out of the One, has come to my couch and eaten at my table?" Yeshua said to her, "I am he who exists out of the Equilibrium. I have been given that which belongs to my Father." "I am your disciple!" "Because of this," I say to you, "whoever comes to be whole, will be full of light. But a divided one will be full of darkness."

Notes

*a. This saying presents many technical and cultural difficulties for translation. The first has to do with **bed** or "couch." It was a custom in the ancient Near East to recline while eating. Since this is a form of "rest" an understandable translation is to make the couch a bed.*

b. Salome's first

QUESTIONS FOR REFLECTION

1. Death continues to be a subject in this saying, but now it is part of a conversation between one of his female students and Yeshua. What wisdom do you find in this saying?
2. What is the meaning of the word **rest** and its two reference points, a bed and a couch?
3. What is the Realm of Unity and what kind of unity does it produce inside a human being?
4. What does "be full of light mean?" What other word, used in other traditions does it suggest?
5. Why do you think Salome suddenly proclaims her commitment to Yeshua? What would bring about such an exclamation in her?
6. What will Yeshua do now that she has become a true student?

Personal Reflections

*statement indicates that she understands Yeshua's origins to be in the one Source, which gives her a certain advantage in interpreting his sayings. Yeshua's reply is to affirm that he comes from the **Realm of Unity**. This phrase translates a word used only once in the Gospel of Thomas, but appears to be in contrast with the word **fragmented** or "divided." As in the academic version, the term could also be translated with words like "equilibrium," "balance," or "whole" understood as a totality or unity.*

*c. When Yeshua says **if you become whole**... the word **whole** in the original is one letter different from the first word **Unity** used above, but which literally means **destroyed**. This would appear to be a scribal error. If it is not then the sentence should read, "If you become destroyed you will be full of light." This seems, however, to be incongruent with the meaning of the rest of the text.*

LOGION 62

Yeshua says,

I disclose my mysteries
to those ready for Mystery
—so keep secret from your left hand
what your right hand is doing.

Academic Translation

Yeshua said, "I speak my mysteries to those who are worthy of my mysteries. Do not let the left realize what the right is doing."

Questions for Reflection

1. What is a mystery? What mysteries has the Gospel of Thomas been telling?
2. How does one prepare for mystery?
3. The significance of the metaphors of right and left hand are part of many cultures. How do you understand these metaphors?
4. What might they symbolize in you, or tell about you?
5. Should one hand dominate another?
6. Is there such a thing as "right- hand thinking" and its opposite, "left-hand thinking?" What is the difference?

Personal Reflections

Notes

a. Interestingly there is a gap in the text having to do with the word **ready**. *It is not clear what this word should be, but based upon other parts of the text either* **ready** *or "worthy" appears to be an appropriate restoration of the text.*

b. The word **hand** *is not in the text, but implied.*

c. **Keep secret** *expresses the literal words "do not let the left realize…."*

LOGION 63

Yeshua says,

There was a rich man
who had expendable wealth.
He said to himself,
"I will take my money
and use it to plant, sow and harvest,
filling my barns with the produce,
then I'll have everything"
— these were the thoughts
occupying his mind.
That night he died.
Listen, if you are paying attention!

Academic Translation

Yeshua said, "There was a wealthy man who possessed many riches. He said, 'I will make use of my money in order to sow, plant, reap, and fill my storehouse with the fruit so that I lack nothing. These were the thoughts of his heart. That night, however, he died. Whoever has ears to hear let them listen."

QUESTIONS FOR REFLECTION

1. Using any of the metaphors found in the previous sayings, describe this man. By using this parable what truth or wisdom is Yeshua illustrating?
2. What in fact is missing for this man who has everything?
3. Are this man's abundant material possessions the problem or something else?
4. What is this man listening to? What else must be heard?
5. In what other ways do you or those around you fail to hear this message?

Personal Reflections

Notes

a. The word **barn** *is literally a "treasure house."*

b. **I will have everything** *translates the literal "so that I do not need anything."*

LOGION 64

Yeshua says,

A man was throwing a dinner party and when everything was prepared, he sent his servant out to call the guests.

The servant went to the first and said,
"My master invites you."
But he replied, "I have set aside some
funds for merchants who are coming
this evening, and I will be placing orders.
I beg to be excused from dinner."

So he went to the second and said,
"My master has invited you."
But he said, "I have bought a house
which requires a day of my time.
I am too busy to come."

He went to another and said to him,
"My master invites you now."
He replied to the servant, "My friend is
getting married and I am to prepare the
wedding banquet.

I simply cannot come.
I beg to be excused."

He went to another and said,
"My master calls you."
In reply he said to the servant,
"I have just bought a farm
and am about to pay taxes.
I cannot come. Please excuse me.
I must be off."

The servant returned to his master and
said, "The ones you invited to the
dinner have all excused themselves."
The master said to the servant, "Then
go to outsiders and strangers on the
roads. Find folk there and
bring them here to eat.
Those busy buying and selling
cannot get into my Father's realm."

Academic Translation

Yeshua said, "A man was having guests and when he had prepared the dinner, he sent his servant out to call them. He went to the first and said to him, 'My master calls you.' He replied, 'I have some funds for some merchants who are coming to me this evening. I will be placing orders with them. I beg to be excused from dinner.' He went to another saying, 'My master has invited you.' He said to him, 'I have bought a house which requires a day of my time. I shall have no respite.' He came to another and said to him, 'My master calls you.' He said to him, 'My friend is getting married and I cannot come for I am making the dinner. I ask you to excuse me.' He went to another one and said, 'My master calls you.' He replied, 'I have bought a farm and am on my way to pay taxes. I cannot come. Please excuse me.' The servant went back and said to his master, 'Those you invited to the dinner have all excused themselves.' The Master said to the servant, 'Go outside and onto the roads. Seize them there and bring them to eat.' Traders and merchants will not enter the place of my father."

QUESTIONS FOR REFLECTION

1. This saying, connected to the one before it and the one which follows, appears to be an illustrative series. Together what do they illustrate about wisdom or its absence?
2. This extensive narrative, the longest in the Gospel of Thomas, gives four instances of refusal to come to the Master's table. How would you describe each refusal? What do they share in common? How are they different?
3. What is the consistent message to each individual?
4. In the context of Yeshua's teaching, who might the outsiders and strangers be?
5. Is business (buying and selling) the real problem, or is it symbolic of something else? What might that be?

Personal Reflections

Notes

a. This narrative reads like a modern conversation. It is universal in tone and approachable. What is different about it, however, is what the master does at the end, inviting strangers to the banquet. Given the circumstances, this appears to be uncommon in any culture.

LOGION 65

Yeshua says,

A good and fair-minded man had a vineyard that he gave over to tenants to work and make productive.
When he sent a servant to
collect profit from the vineyard,
the tenants took him and nearly
beat him to death.
When the servant returned he told his
master who said, "Perhaps they
did not know him."
So he sent another servant
and they beat him as well.
Then the master said, "I'll send my son.
Maybe that will shame them."
But those tenants, because they knew
him to be heir to the vineyard,
seized and killed him.
Whoever can hear this, listen!

Academic Translation

Yeshua said, "An upright man had a vineyard which he gave over to tenants to work and collect its fruits. He sent a servant to collect produce from the vineyard, but the tenants took and beat him, almost killing him. The servant returned and told his master who said, 'Perhaps he did not know them.' He sent another servant but the tenants beat him as well. It was then that the master sent his son saying, 'Perhaps because of my son they will be ashamed of themselves.' But knowing that he was heir to the vineyard, the tenants took him and killed him. Whoever has ears for this must listen."

Notes

a. The translation of this text is fairly straightforward

QUESTIONS FOR REFLECTION

1. If this is a story about humanity, or about the Hebrew people representing humanity, what does this say about the "fair-minded man," and about the ones he sent to collect profit?
2. What is the fair-minded man's intentions?
3. Why would the tenants act as they did? Why are they hostile? What is their problem? Are they simply malicious?
4. If this story is connected to the ones which came before it, what is the link? What is the condition of humanity described by these parables?
5. What do the individuals in these stories reject?

Personal Reflections

except for one phrase, translated above, in the academic version literally, "Perhaps he did not know them." This is a puzzling line which may suggest a scribal error, or it could point toward a much more nuanced understanding of the text. If the original version is not an error, then the master's reply, appears to put blame (or responsibility) for the tenants' reaction on the servant (he)—his lack of understanding of them. However, from what the rest of the texts suggests, this interpretation seems to be unwarranted. The tenants are entirely misguided.

b. The more conventional translation **Perhaps they did not know him** is used in the dynamic version.

LOGION 66

Yeshua says,

Bring me the stone
   the builders discarded.
   That one will be the key.

Academic Translation

Yeshua says, "Show me the stone the builders cast off. That one is the keystone."

QUESTIONS FOR REFLECTION

1. We are each builders in some way. We are building our lives, stories, and dreams. The question is, of course, what are we including in our structures and what are we leaving out? What materials are we using, and which are being excluded?
2. What would you say you are building? What materials are you using?
3. Are you leaving anything out by discarding some key element?
4. Yeshua seems to think we may be overlooking some key. What could it be?

Personal Reflections

Notes

a. This saying, familiar to us from the canonical Gospels, can be variously translated, but each one with the same intent.

b. The term **discarded** *can be translated as "turned down," "cast away," "rejected," "abandoned."*

c. In both ancient and modern building practice a "key stone" locks other stones in place, or provides a gauge for the rest of the building.

LOGION 67

Yeshua says,

I f you come to know all,
   and yet you yourself are lacking,
   you have missed everything.

Academic Translation

Yeshua said, "If the one who knows 'the All' is personally deficient, then that one lacks everything."

Notes

a. This short saying presents interesting challenges for the translator. The first is the word **all** or "the All." This term is important in Greek usage. It is used in St. Paul's Epistles to signify the Totality (all things), thought of as a cognate for the Semitic term that encompasses the realm of the Kingdom. (In other words, when the

QUESTIONS FOR REFLECTION

1. What kind of knowledge is Yeshua talking about? What is our definition of "all?"
2. How can the "self" be lacking? What could be missing or absent from the self?
3. The following formula "knowing all but suffering absence in the self = zero—the dearth of everything" might be one way to understand this saying. Is there some other way you might rewrite this formula?

Personal Reflections

Hebrew tradition uses the word "Kingdom," the Greeks would typically use "the All" as was done in this saying).

b. The phrase **you yourself are lacking** (or "personally deficient") translates the literal "if he lacks himself."

c. The final phrase **missed everything** (or "lacks everything") translates "lacks the place of the All." The term "place" appears to signify the actuality or reality of the Whole.

LOGION 68

Yeshua says,

Blessed are you who
in the midst of persecution,
when they hate
and pursue you
even to the core of your being,
cannot find "you" anywhere.

Academic Translation

Yeshua said, "Blessed are you when they reject and persecute you, but cannot discover you anywhere in those places where they persecute you right down into your being."

QUESTIONS FOR REFLECTION

1. Similar in tone and content to the Beatitudes in the Sermon on the Mount, Yeshua more fully explores the experience of persecution, hate, and pursuit. In this saying where does persecution take place? Where does it conclude?
2. What does the last phrase in the saying mean? It seems strange, particularly in light of the previous logion. How would you interpret this saying, and then put the two together?
3. Why would it be a "blessing" not to find "you" at the core of being?

Personal Reflections

Notes

a. This saying, though it appears odd in translation, seems to express an understanding of an absence (or finding the place of persecution empty), when one is pursued down into the depths of being without being "seized upon" (which is the recurring word from the first logion).

LOGION 69

Yeshua says,

Blessed are all those
persecuted right into
the depths of the heart.
Only there will they come to know
their true Father and Source.
Blessed are the hungry ones.
Their inner longings will be satisfied.

Academic Translation

Yeshua said, "Blessed are those pursued right into the depths of their hearts. It is there that they have the Father in truth. Blessed are the hungry, their womb of longing will be filled."

QUESTIONS FOR REFLECTION

1. Similar in subject and in tone to the previous saying, this one takes the matter to an even deeper level and creates a double blessing. How are the blessings related to each other in this logion, and to the previous saying?
2. How might these sayings be related to Logion 66?
3. How does persecution prepare the heart to find the true Father and Source?
4. How could such an experience produce both hungering and satisfaction?
5. What might the results of such an experience be?

Personal Reflections

Notes

a. The Greek word **persecuted** could just as easily be translated "pursued."

b. The term **true Father** is literally as the academic version presents it above. However, it is also possible to translate it as "they have known the truth of the Father."

c. The final phrase appears to be purely idiomatic in Coptic expressing deep-seated desire or longing.

LOGION 70

Yeshua says,

When you give birth
to that which is
within yourself;
what you bring forth will save you.
If you possess nothing within,
that absence will destroy you.

Academic Translation

Yeshua said, "When you bring into being that which is in yourself, what you have will save you. If you do not have anything within, what you do not have will kill you."

QUESTIONS FOR REFLECTION

1. In the context of the previous sayings, this logion is clearly paradoxical. What is the paradox that is being highlighted?
2. What does the image of "giving birth" suggest?
3. How would this infant be able to save you?
4. How is absence destructive? What absence are we talking about?

Personal Reflections

Notes

a. The impact of this saying is felt in either version. In the original text, the absence is objectified by saying that missing "thing" which you do not have will kill you.

LOGION 71

Yeshua says,

I will destroy this house
and no one will ever
be able to rebuild it.

Academic Translation

Yeshua said, "I will destroy this house and no one can build (it)."

QUESTIONS FOR REFLECTION

1. Following directly from the previous saying, destruction is once again mentioned in this logion. Are these forms of destructions the same?
2. What is "this house" that Yeshua is talking about?
3. Why is Yeshua involved?
4. How does destruction usually take place? Is that the way Yeshua will do it?

Personal Reflections

a. In the original text there appears to be a phrase missing that might indicate "rebuilding" or building it back again.

LOGION 72

A man said to Yeshua,

Speak to my brothers
    so that they will divide
    my father's belongings
with me."

Yeshua replied to him,
"Sir, who has made me the divider?"

He turned to his students and asked,
"Am I here to divide?"

Academic Translation

A man said to Yeshua, "Speak to my brothers so that they will divide the possessions of my father with me." Yeshua said to him, "O man, who is it that made me a divider?" He turned to his students and asked, "Do I truly exist to be a divider?"

QUESTIONS FOR REFLECTION

1. Is there a relationship between the process of division and destruction?
2. Why does the man in this saying want Yeshua to be a judge and arbiter?
3. What answer should Yeshua's student's give to his question of them?
4. How would you answer, taking Logion 16 into consideration?
5. What is Yeshua here to do? How would you answer that question?

Personal Reflections

Notes

a. The word **divide** and **divider** could possibly be translated with terms such as "apportion" and "arbiter." However, there is a play throughout the text on the contrast between uniting and dividing, which appears to be the issue Yeshua focuses upon.

LOGION 73

Yeshua says,

The harvest is abundant.
The reapers are few.
Implore the Master of Harvest
to send out workers.

Academic Translation

Yeshua said, "The harvest is plentiful indeed, but there are few laborers. Pray, therefore, to the Lord to send laborers into the harvest."

QUESTIONS FOR REFLECTION

1. This saying echoes ones in the canonical Gospels and the images of seed-planting and harvest found throughout the Gospel texts. If harvest-time is at the "end of the ages" (as was suggested earlier), is this the same harvest?
2. Why are there few reapers?
3. Who is the master of the harvest? How might that prayer be answered by Yeshua?
4. Notice that this and the next two sayings appear to be related. What is their relationship?

Personal Reflections

Notes

a. **Master of the Harvest** *is literally "the Lord" and may be conventionally understood as God (known as the unnamable "Yahweh") in the Hebrew tradition.*

LOGION 74

Yeshua says,

O Lord,
   many have gathered
   around the fountain,
but there is nothing in the well.

Academic Translation

Yeshua said, "Lord, there are many around the fountain, but there is nothing in the well."

QUESTIONS FOR REFLECTION

1. This saying appears to be one of Yeshua's own prayers. Why might this and the prayer mentioned in the logion before be his prayers?
2. If he is acknowledging a fact in this prayer. What has he observed?
3. What is the meaning of this observation? What might this saying be about in our world?
4. What then is he praying for?
5. How might the answer to his prayer, also remedy the concerns he has just expressed?
6. How might the images used in this saying relate to the ones which are expressed in the next?

Personal Reflections

Notes

a. The word **fountain** *can be thought of as a drinking fountain or even spring, but the last word makes it clear that it is meant to hold water but does not.*

Logion 75

Yeshua says,

Many are standing
    at the door,
        but only the single
or solitary will enter the place of union.

Academic Translation

Yeshua said, "There are many standing at the door, but only those who are single will enter the place of marriage."

QUESTIONS FOR REFLECTION

1. What is Yeshua talking about when he speaks of the "place of union?"
2. How has the theme of the single or solitary been expressed before?
3. What does "single" mean?
4. Why cannot "many" enter this chamber, only the "single one."
5. What is a single one?
6. How does entry occur?

Personal Reflections

Notes

a. The phrase **single and solitary** translates the literal term **monachos** used previously (Logion 16 and 49).

b. **Place of union** is literally "the place of marriage" or, perhaps it might also be translated as the "bridal chamber." What is at issue here is that this place represents the chamber where union takes place.

LOGION 76

Yeshua says,

The Father's Realm
can be compared to
a merchant who discovered
a pearl hidden in a consignment
of goods. Wisely, he returned the goods
and bought the single pearl instead.

You too must seek out
for yourselves an enduring treasure
in that realm where moths
cannot get in to eat
or insects come to destroy.

Academic Translation

Yeshua said, "The kingdom of the Father can be compared with a merchant who discovered a pearl in a consignment of goods. The merchant was wise. He returned the goods and bought the lone pearl for himself. You yourself must seek out an enduring treasure that does not perish in that place where no moth can come in to eat, nor worm go to destroy."

QUESTIONS FOR REFLECTION

1. In one version or another, this is a well known saying of Yeshua's where he uses the image of the "pearl of great price" as an important metaphor. In this context what does it mean?
2. There are interesting contrasts in the way Yeshua speaks of merchants. Compare this saying to Logion 64. What is the contrast? Why is this important?
3. Notice again the emphasis Yeshua places upon seeking the treasure out for one's self? This raises the questions: what is the treasure one is looking for? Where does one go to find it?
4. Where is the realm in which the treasure is found?
5. What is the "enduring treasure?" How would you describe it?

Personal Reflections

Notes

*a. One of the significant words in this saying is the **single** pearl. Use of this word puts emphasis upon the unitary nature of the pearl.*

*b. The word **seek** is the same which is used in Logion 2 and informs the basis of all action in this Gospel.*

LOGION 77

Yeshua says,

I am the light
shining upon all things.
I am the sum of everything,
for everything has come forth from me,
and towards me everything unfolds.
Split a piece of wood,
and there I am.
Pick up a stone
and you will find me there.

Academic Translation

Yeshua said, "I am the light which shines upon all things. I am the All. The All has come out of me and the All extends back to me. Split a timber, and I am is there. Lift a stone and you will discover me there."

Notes

a. Many aspects of this saying are significant and suggestive. First, the use of the term **I am** *which echoes the Hebrew tradition of the Presence of the I Am before Moses in the desert. It is also reflective of the same usage particularly in St. John's Gospel where Yeshua speaks with the authority of the I Am.*

b. The second significant term is the repeated use of **the All** *which is the Greek term for the Totality of everything, which can be understood as a cognate for the*

QUESTIONS FOR REFLECTION

1. Of all the sayings recorded in the Gospel of Thomas, this one has, perhaps, the most Eastern feel. However, it is also very Semitic in tone because of the use of the phrase I AM (which is Hebraic code for the divine Presence which appeared at the burning bush in Moses' experience). How does this saying touch you?
2. Who is speaking in this saying?
3. What is the light?
4. This saying presents direct metaphysical descriptions of Reality in an almost Zen-like way. Draw a diagram to illustrate the content of these descriptions. Do you see anything differently as a result? What?
5. What is the significance of the use of the images of wood and stone?
6. Is matter a barrier to the divine Presence?
7. Where did Moses go to find the divine Presence? Where must you go to seek that same Presence?

Personal Reflections

Kingdom in Semitic terminology.

c. The interesting phraseology **and towards me everything unfolds** *seeks to express a word that literally means "split open" but seems to carry the connotation of opening or unfolding. The same word is used in the phrase* **split a piece of wood.**

d. In the final phrase lifting a stone allows one to **find,** *"discover" (or "seize upon") the Presence of the I Am.*

Logion 78

Yeshua says,

Why did you come out
into the wilderness?
To see a reed
blown about by the wind?
A man dressed in soft raiment
like your rulers and the powerful?
Yes, indeed, they are clothed in fine,
luxurious garments,
but what they lack
is the ability to discern truth.

Academic Translation

Yeshua said, "Why did you come out into the desert? To see a reed moved by the wind? To see a man wearing soft garments like your kings and those in power? Indeed they are clothed in soft apparel but they know nothing of the truth."

QUESTIONS FOR REFLECTION

1. What is the wilderness in this saying? Is it a Middle Eastern desert, or some other place?
2. What two kinds of beings reside in this desert, though one of them is only alluded to by contrast?
3. Using the words of this saying, describe the other being or presence in the wilderness.
4. Here is an image of someone who has it all, and yet lacks something vital. Why is that lack so important?
5. What is the discernment of truth? How would you describe or define it?

Personal Reflections

Notes

a. The words **ability to discern** translates a significant word for knowing that encompasses concepts like discernment and understanding.

LOGION 79

A woman in the crowd said to him,

Fortunate is the womb
which bore you,
and the breasts
which nourished you."

Yeshua turned to her and said,
"The ones who hear
the Father's Word
and guard its truth
are truly fortunate.
But the days are coming
when you will say,
'Lucky is the womb that never bore,
and the breasts that never gave milk!'"

Academic Translation

A woman in the throng said to him, "Happy is the womb that bore you and the breasts that nursed you." He said to her, "Happy are those who listen to the word of the Father and watch over it in truth. There will be days ahead when you will say, 'Fortunate is the womb that never conceived and the breasts which never gave milk.'"

QUESTIONS FOR REFLECTION

1. What truth has the woman in the crowd discerned?
2. What is this greater discernment of truth about?
3. What does it mean to guard truth as the Father's Word?
4. This and the previous logion remind us of the apocalyptic sayings of both John and Yeshua. What future vision of the world or experience of the cosmos might these be about?

Personal Reflections

Notes

a. The word **fortunate** is often translated as "blessed" but this confuses the term with **makarios** which is the designation used in Thomas and in the canonical Gospels for specific beatitudes. Here the word is different and signifies fortune or luck that creates happiness.

b. The **Father's word** is literally the "**logos** of the Father" which clearly signifies something more than mere words or speaking.

c. **Guard** is the same word used in Logion 10 signifying care and protection of something.

LOGION 80

Yeshua says,

Whoever knows the cosmos
discovers the body,
but the cosmos
does not deserve the one
who makes that discovery.

Academic Translation

Yeshua said, "Whoever has known the cosmos has discovered the body. The cosmos is not worthy of the one who has discovered the body."

QUESTIONS FOR REFLECTION

1. What is the nature of the cosmos? What is its function or analogue, according to this logion?
2. What would that function or analogue actually mean?
3. How do most inhabitants of the cosmos understand it?
4. What is different about the one who knows the cosmos to be a body, and someone who never makes this discovery?

Personal Reflections

Notes

a. The word **discovers** *is the same significant term "seize upon" that is used in the opening and subsequent logia.*

b. **Deserve** *could also mean "adequate for, ready for, or worthy of" signifying a superior understanding.*

LOGION 81

Yeshua says,

L et whoever
        becomes rich
        be king,
but let whoever holds power
surrender it.

Academic Translation

Yeshua said, "Whoever becomes rich, let them be king. Whoever has power, let them relinquish it."

QUESTIONS FOR REFLECTION

1. Which of the two individuals described in the previous logion might this saying be about?
2. What progression of spiritual understanding does this describe?
3. What sort of riches is Yeshua talking about? What sort of power?
4. Why would power need to be surrendered?
5. What might happen to the individual who surrenders power?

Personal Reflections

a. The word **surrender** *could also be translated as "renounce," "abdicate," or "abandon."*

LOGION 82

Yeshua says,

Whoever comes
close to me
dwells near the fire.
Whoever moves away from me
remains far from the kingdom.

Academic Translation

Yeshua said, "Whoever is close to me is close to the fire. Whoever is far from me is far from the King-dom."

QUESTIONS FOR REFLECTION

1. The image of fire has been used a number of times in this text. Is there any saying preceding this that would help to explain what this first statement is about?
2. What does it mean to dwell near the fire?
3. What is the experience of those who live near the fire?
4. The verbs used in this logion are very significant. How would you describe or draw them?
5. A king is mentioned in the previous saying and a kingdom spoken about here. What is their relationship?
6. What is the relationship of fire and the kingdom to one another?

Personal Reflections

Notes

a. The words **draws close** and **remains far** translate two words of proximity or immediacy in relationship to Yeshua.

LOGION 83

Yeshua says,

Images are revealed
to humanity while the
light within them is hidden
by the brilliance of
the Father's light.
It is God who is being revealed,
but the image of God
remains concealed
by the blaze of light.

Academic Translation

Yeshua said, "Images are made manifest to humanity and the light within them is hidden in the image of the light of the Father. God will be made manifest, but the divine image is hidden away by means of the light."

QUESTIONS FOR REFLECTION

1. Icons became very significant in Christian imagery and worship. The word icon is used here as a manifestation of light. How do you understand iconography? Is it related to or different from this saying?
2. This saying expresses a complex set of ideas having to do with revelation and concealment, all related to light itself. How can light conceal something? How does light reveal something?
3. What is the "image of God?" In what ways might this phrase be understood?
4. What might be the actual iconic images revealing God to humanity?

Personal Reflections

Notes

a. It is important, first, to note that the word **image** *is literally* **ikon**, *of significance in the early Christian tradition, and also significant to the Hebrew tradition as well since human beings are said to be made in the divine image.*

b. For the entire logion the Coptic phraseology in the original text seems to be somewhat obscure. The word **brilliance** *substitutes for the word "image" which is said to be hidden in the light of God. The dynamic version seems to make more sense to us when translated in this way (with the substitution), but this may expose our inability to understand its semantic complexity, rather than expressing a difficulty in the text itself.*

LOGION 84

Yeshua says,

When you see
your own projection
into time and space
it makes you happy.
But when the time comes
that you are able to look
upon the icon of your own being,
which came into existence
at the beginning,
and neither dies
nor has yet been fully revealed,
will you be able to stand it?

Academic Translation

Yeshua said, "When you observe your own likeness in time you rejoice. But when you come to look upon your image which came into being at the beginning, and neither dies nor fully appears, will you be able to bear it?"

QUESTIONS FOR REFLECTION

1. The cosmological and anthropological implications of this logion are significant. What do you understand them to be? What does it say about you and about the nature of the cosmos?
2. How is this understanding different from the ordinary way we think about reality?
3. Where would the icon of your own being reside?
4. Why is it impossible to look upon it at one point, and at another be able to see it? What would make that difference?
5. What does the last phrase suggest? Is it a negative or a positive statement?
6. What might have to change on the inside in order to gain the vision of our iconic nature?
7. How does this saying describe an icon?
8. What does "at the beginning" mean? Where has the revelation of the icon taken place so far? Will there be more?

Personal Reflections

Notes

a. This saying is most provocative. There is a distinction made between image and likeness (icon of your being and projection).

b. The words into space and time translate the words "(in) the days," meaning in the experience of temporality.

c. The words stand it (or "bear it") may literally mean "wear it."

LOGION 85

Yeshua says,

Adam came into being
        out of a great power
        and fullness,
and yet he is not superior to you.
Had he been prepared for it,
he would not have tasted death.

Academic Translation

Yeshua said, "Adam came into existence out of great power and richness, and yet he was not worthy of you. Had he been deserving he would not have tasted death."

QUESTIONS FOR REFLECTION

1. According to this saying who is superior and who is inferior?
2. What criteria are used to determine superiority and inferiority?
3. What preparation did Adam not have that an individual might have today?
4. From what power and fullness did Adam emerge?
5. Where did he "taste death?"
6. Where can we taste life? What will give us the taste of life?
7. How does one prepare now in a manner that Adam did not or could not? What inner state is necessary for this preparation?

Personal Reflections

Notes

a. There are two key words used in the original text that refer to superiority or greatness and can mean worthy or deserving. They can speak also about a state of readiness or adequacy.

LOGION 86

Yeshua says,

Foxes have dens
and birds have nests,
    but the son of humanity
has no place to lay his head and rest.

Academic Translation

Yeshua said, "Foxes have their dens and birds their nests, but there is no place for the son of humanity to lay his head and rest himself."

QUESTIONS FOR REFLECTION

1. What are dens for foxes and nests for birds?
2. Where does the son of humanity rest?
3. Might there be other ways of saying this logion? Rewrite it in your own words.
4. How might this familiar saying illustrate the previous Logion 81?
5. Imagine that this saying is a commentary on the previous pairing of "movement" and "rest?" What does it suggest?

Personal Reflections

Notes

a. It may be significant to emphasize, as some traditions do, the place called "no place" as suggested in the academic version.

LOGION 87

Yeshua says,

Miserable is the body
that depends upon a body,
and the soul
that depends upon both.

Academic Translation

Yeshua said, "Wretched is the body that depends upon a body, and wretched is the soul that depends upon both."

QUESTIONS FOR REFLECTION

1. Could this saying be the reason why Yeshua has no place to lay his head? If that is a possible interpretation, what might this logion mean?
2. What does dependency mean?
3. There are three possible forms of dependency (or independence) suggested by this saying. What are they and what do they suggest?
4. If this saying were turned into one suggesting blessing, how might it read?
5. Is there any higher authority than the body or the soul? Do body and soul have the last word? If not, then who or what does?

Personal Reflections

Notes

a. The term **miserable** *(or "wretched") can also be translated as a hardship or a calamity, and may contrast with "blessed."*

LOGION 88

Yeshua says,

The angels and the prophets
will come and bring you
what already belongs to you,
and you will give to them
what you have to give.
But ask yourself this:
When may they come
and receive back from you
what already belongs to them?

Academic Translation

Yeshua said, "The angels and the prophets will come to you, and give you those things that are yours, and you will give them what you have to give. But ask yourselves this, on what day may they come and take what is theirs?"

QUESTIONS FOR REFLECTION

1. This saying raises many new and interesting questions about humans and the cosmos we inhabit. Among the first is, what role do angels and prophets play in the universe and in a person's life?
2. What could angels and prophets bring that we do not already have, and yet which belongs to us?
3. What do we have that we can give to them? What do we have that belongs to them? This second question appears to be different from the first.
4. What are we getting ready in this life?

Personal Reflections

Notes

a. This saying concerns exchange, the giving and receiving of those things which one either already has or which belong to the individual.

LOGION 89

Yeshua says,

For what reason would you
only wash
the outside of a cup?
Do you not realize
that the creator of the outside
is the one who made the inside as well?

Academic Translation

Yeshua said, "For what reason would you only wash the outside of the cup? Do you not understand that whoever created the inside also created the outside?"

QUESTIONS FOR REFLECTION

1. Yeshua shifts the emphasis in his sacred tradition. How and why does he do this?
2. What are these metaphors about?
3. What is the significance of the cup?
4. In what ways might one wash the inside of the cup?

Personal Reflections

Notes

a. The word **realize** *is not the common word "know" but a word that has to do in Greek with awareness through the inner Intellect or* **nous***.*

LOGION 90

Yeshua says,

Come to me
for justice is my yoke,
and gentleness is my rule,
and you will discover the state of rest.

Academic Translation

Yeshua said, "Come to me for my yoke is fair, and my lordship is gentle, and you will seize upon rest."

QUESTIONS FOR REFLECTION

1. Justice and gentleness are said to be two aspects of discipleship under Yeshua as Master. How would you describe these? How might they be different from one another and how do they work together?
2. What is the meaning of yoke and rule? How do you understand and interpret these? More importantly, how might one experience these?
3. Together they lead to the state of rest that has been highlighted in this text a number of times. How would justice and gentleness help one discover a state of rest?
4. How do you come to know these facets of Yeshua's rule?

Personal Reflections

Notes

a. There are many significant semantic details in this saying. The first has to do with the word **justice**. It is the same word used in Logion 65 for the fair-minded man.

b. Translating the original word **rule** (or "lord-ship") is difficult without using one in English that suggests an opposite meaning for the phrase or is rhetorically awkward. The original word for **rule** is often translated as "Lord" or "Teacher" but it has to do more with the rule or guidance of a Master. This is an invitation to experience two aspects of the Master's guidance which then allows an individual to "seize upon" or discover the final **state of rest** mentioned in Logion 2 and elsewhere (Logia 50, 51, and 60).

LOGION 91

They said to him,

Tell us who you
really are so we
may believe in you."

He said to them,
"You have learned to read
the face of earth and sky,
but you do not yet recognize
the one standing in your presence,
nor can you make sense of
the present moment."

Academic Translation

They said to him, "Tell us who you are so that we may believe you." He said to them, "You can read the face of the earth and the sky, but you do not know the one who is present before you, nor do you know how to read this very moment."

Questions for Reflection

1. From the questions which his students ask him, can you tell anything about their inner state or level of learning?
2. What are they really asking him?
3. From Yeshua's answer how would you describe his shift of emphasis?
4. Yeshua identifies two important aspects of knowing him as Master. How would you describe these?
5. What is the significance of the present moment?

Personal Reflections

Notes

a. The phrase **standing in your presence** *is similar to the phrase "the one in the Presence before you" in Logion 5.*

b. There is a contrast made between **read** *and* **recognize** *(or "know").*

c. The word for **present moment** *is kairos, having to do with time understood as the "proper moment" or the "right time."*

LOGION 92

Yeshua says,

Seek now, I say,
and you will find
that for which you search.
You see, I am ready to tell you
everything you were asking earlier
and did not explain,
but at the moment
no one is searching out anything.

Yeshua said, "Seek
and you will find,
for it is my desire
to tell you now
those things which
you asked before
and I did not
answer, but you are
not seeking after
them."

QUESTIONS FOR REFLECTION

1. In this logion we have returned full circle to a number of different elements described earlier in the teaching. What are they?
2. Why would this be the moment for a fuller disclosure than before?
3. Yeshua describes the inner state of his students. His statement follows directly from the previous where they are indeed seeking an answer. Are these two sayings incompatible? How could they be seeking and Yeshua still be correct in his assessment of their search?
4. Where should one search? In which direction?
5. What would inhibit the search or prevent the finding?

Personal Reflections

a. The phrase **I am ready** *translates "it is my desire," or more literally, "it pleases me."*

LOGION 93

Yeshua says,

Do not give what is sacred to dogs who will only discard it on a manure pile. Do not cast pearls in front of pigs who will only trample and ruin them.

**Academic
Translation**

Yeshua said, "Do
not give dogs what
is holy so that they
throw it away on
the dung heap. Do
not cast pearls to
the pigs for that
they will (trample)
them."

QUESTIONS FOR REFLECTION

1. In a previous logion (88) Yeshua has spoken about the need to give things away.
   There it was a positive. Here it is a negative?
   What kind of "giving" is this?
2. What kind of giving do we do?
3. Who or what are the dogs and the pigs?
   These are clearly unclean animals in Jewish
   tradition. What would be unclean for
   Yeshua?

Personal Reflections

Notes

a. The words
**trample and
ruin** *are implied
by a break in the
text.*

LOGION 94

Yeshua says,

Those seeking will find
what they are looking for.
Doors will swing open
for the ones who knock.

Academic Translation

Yeshua said, "The one who seeks will find, and they will open the door for the one who knocks."

QUESTIONS FOR REFLECTION

1. Like logion 93, this saying repeats a familiar theme also found in the canonical Gospels. What is the emphasis here?
2. Does the fact that it is placed here in the text change its meaning in any way?
3. What do the second set of metaphors suggest?
4. What sort of knocking is required?

Personal Reflections

Notes

a. There is a break in the text where the word "knock" perhaps should be.

LOGION 95

Yeshua says,

If you have money,
     do not lend it at interest.
     Give it instead
to those from whom you
cannot take it back.

Academic Translation

Yeshua said, "If you have money do not give it with interest, rather give it to those from whom you cannot not take it back."

QUESTIONS FOR REFLECTION

1. What kind of person is Yeshua describing? Who would do this sort of thing?
2. What is required on the inside of a person in order to act in this way?
3. In Logion 93 Yeshua has counseled that a person should withhold giving? Here the action is reversed. What is the difference?
4. What kind of freedom is Yeshua describing?
5. What is the result of such giving?

Personal Reflections

Notes

a. The opening word suggests that many who hear this will not have any money at all.

LOGION 96

Yeshua says,

The Father's realm
can be compared
to a woman
who takes a tiny bit of yeast,
folds it into dough
and makes great loaves
out of it.
Whoever has ears for this, listen!

Academic Translation

Yeshua said, "The kingdom of the Father is like a woman who took a small amount of yeast, concealed it in dough, and made it into large loaves. Whoever has ears, listen!"

QUESTIONS FOR REFLECTION

1. Bread making is considered a sacred act in the Middle East. Yeshua uses this basic work which meets the needs of humanity to also describe the Kingdom. What form of yeast is Yeshua talking about?
2. What happens to yeast? What happens in the Kingdom?
3. What should we learn from this?
4. How is our work like the woman's, and how do we get ready for it?

Personal Reflections

Notes

a. The term **compared to** has been used extensively in this text expressing analogy or contrast.

b. The word **folds** expressed the implied verb which is believed to be "hid" or "concealed" but is a blank spot in the text.

LOGION 97

Yeshua says,

The Father's realm
        is like a woman carrying
        a jar full of meal.
While she is walking on a path
some distance from her home,
the handle of her jug breaks,
and the meal spills out
behind her on the road.
She is unaware of the problem,
for she has noticed nothing.
When she opens the door
of her house
and puts the jar down,
suddenly she discovers it empty.

Academic Translation

Yeshua said, "The Father's Kingdom is comparable to a woman carrying a jar full of flour. Walking on the road far from her home the ear of the jar broke and the flour emptied out behind her on the road. She did not know it, for she had not noticed the problem. When she entered her house and put the jar down, she discovered it empty."

QUESTIONS FOR REFLECTION

1. This and the previous logion are linked, but they appear to be opposite images, though both are about providing for the necessities of a household in buying meal and baking bread. How do they each illustrate the principles governing the Father's realm?
2. Are these logion complimentary opposites?
3. How should this second parable be interpreted? If you imagine that the picture of the empty jar is a negative image, what would that mean? If instead, you imagine it to be positive, how would that change your interpretation? Try both approaches. Which one do you think is correct?
4. Should the woman have noticed the accident? What does the fact that she did not suggest to you?
5. What is the significance of the words about walking the path?
6. How is emptiness a sign of the Kingdom? Why might it be necessary?

Personal Reflections

Notes

a. The words **from her home** *are implied but not written in the text.*

LOGION 98

Yeshua says,

The Father's realm
is like a man wanting
to kill someone powerful.
So he draws a sword
in his own house and
puts it through the wall
to test whether or not
his hand is actually strong enough.
Then he goes out and slays the giant.

Academic Translation

Yeshua said, "The Kingdom of the Father is like a man wanting to kill a man of power. He drew the sword in his own home and thrust it into the wall to find out if his hand was innately strong, and then he killed the powerful one."

QUESTIONS FOR REFLECTION

1. This third parable in a series about the Kingdom, speaks to another principle. What is this principle about?
2. Where does the man draw the sword? Where does he slay the giant?
3. What is the giant— the powerful person? Why must the giant be killed?
4. What does **killing** mean?

Personal Reflections

Notes

a. The dynamic version is rendered into a more colloquial text, especially with the use of the word **giant** – which may be metaphorically but not literally correct. The **powerful** person is perhaps in reference to persons of power referred to in Logion 78.

b. The term **strong enough** is literally "inwardly strong" in the original text.

LOGION 99

His students said to him,

Your brothers and
your mother are standing
just outside the door."

"My true mother and brothers
are those present right here
who fulfill my Father's desires.
It is they who will get into
my Father's realm," he replied.

Academic Translation

His students said to him, "Your mother and brothers are standing on the outside." He said to them, "Those here in this place who do the will of my Father are my brothers and my mother. It is they who will go inside my Father's Kingdom."

QUESTIONS FOR REFLECTION

1. This and the following logia appear to be about right relationships with others who either are or are not on their way into the kingdom. How does Yeshua define the relationship to mothers and brothers?
2. Is the place they are standing of significance?
3. From Yeshua's point of view what distinguishes a true relationship from a false one?
4. What are the Father's desires? How does one fulfill them?

Personal Reflections

Notes

a. The contrast between those on the outside and those on the inside is emphasized by the way this saying is constructed.

b. The word **desires** *is the same as the word used in the previous saying concerning the man's desire to use the sword against the powerful.*

LOGION 100

They showed him a gold coin and said,

Caesar's agents
demand tribute
from us."

He said to them,
"Then give to Caesar
what is Caesar's.
Give to God
what is God's.
And give me
that which is mine."

**Academic
Translation**

The showed Yeshua
a gold coin and
said to him, "Those
belonging to
Caesar demand
taxes from us." He
replied, "Give
Caesar what is
Caesar's, give God
what is God's and
give me what is
mine."

QUESTIONS FOR REFLECTION

1. Yeshua very clearly outlines three domains
    and their authority. How would you define
    these domains and what relationship do
    they have to one another?
2. What do you feel needs to be given in each
    domain?
3. Should anything be withheld?

Personal Reflections

Notes

a. **Tribute** *is
understood to be
taxes. A construc-
tion is used in the
original which
expresses those
things that belong
either to one
person or another.*

LOGION 101

Yeshua says,

Whoever does not reject
father and mother
in the way I do
cannot be my student.
Whoever does not welcome
father and mother as I do
cannot be my disciple,
for my mother brought me forth,
but Truth gave me life.

Academic Translation

Yeshua said, "Whoever does not hate father and mother in the way I do cannot be my student. Whoever does not love father and mother in the way I do cannot be my student. For my mother begot me but (my true mother) gave me life."

QUESTIONS FOR REFLECTION

1. This saying is both like (and unlike) ones in the canonical Gospels. What are the similarities and differences?
2. Using the notes, examine the various ways this saying could be translated. If you changed the translation would you need to change the interpretation?
3. What does **reject** and **welcome** (or **accept** mean)? How has Yeshua demonstrated both concepts?
4. Is he talking about natural parents or something else?
5. Yeshua often speaks of the the Father as his origin, but here he balances the masculine image with a feminine one. In this case what would the feminine symbolize?

Personal Reflections

Notes

a. There are several difficulties of translation in this text. The first is one encountered in several logia prior to this (Logion 43, 55, and 68) having to do with the words "hate" and "love." Various translations of this word are used to draw out multiple meanings semantically possible.

b. There are also several lacuna (or gaps) in this text. The first has to do with the term, **brought me forth**. Forth is in the text but **brought me** is missing.

c. Furthermore, the word **Truth** stands by itself in the Coptic text, but it is conventionally translated as "my true mother." Whether this is warranted or not is not entirely clear.

LOGION 102

Yeshua says,

Cursed are your
religious leaders
for they are like dogs
sleeping in the feed bin.
They do not eat
nor do they allow
the cattle to eat.

Academic Translation

Yeshua said, "Woe to the Pharisees for they are like a dog asleep in the manger. It does not eat, nor does it permit the cattle to eat."

QUESTIONS FOR REFLECTION

1. Yeshua does not seem to have a high regard for some of the religious leaders of his day. What appears to be the problem?
2. Eating and feeding have been important concepts in previous sayings. What kind of food is Yeshua talking about?
3. What does the fact that dogs do not eat what cattle eat have to do with this saying?
4. A curse is the opposite of what?
5. How else would you describe the religious leaders Yeshua is talking about?

Personal Reflections

Notes

a. The **feed bin** *is the feeding trough for cattle. The word* **allow** *is missing from the text, but implied and reconstructed.*

LOGION 103

Yeshua says,

Blessed are those aware
of the approach of thieves,
who know when and where
they will enter before they appear,
for then they can arise and prepare
by gathering their sovereignty
about them,
binding to themselves
that which was from the beginning.

**Academic
Translation**

Yeshua said,
"Blessed is the man
who knows where
the thieves will
enter, so before
they come in he
may rise and gather
his domain about
him, binding upon
his loins that
which was from
the beginning."

QUESTIONS FOR REFLECTION

1. What kind of blessing and what form of knowledge is Yeshua talking about in this logion?
2. How would a person come to know when and where a thief was entering? Supposedly thieves can do their work exactly because they act in secret.
3. The form of knowledge that Yeshua is talking about allows for a particular kind of action. How would you describe that action?
4. What is the actor (or blessed person) doing in this logion?
5. In what way are these elements being gathered?

Personal Reflections

Notes

a. A number of important translation issues are present in this text. The first is an ambiguity about either where (in what place) or when (at what time) the thieves will come in.

b. The text literally says that he will gather his "kingdom" to himself, which suggests that **sovereignty** *may be the best translation. Both the dynamic and academic versions stay close to the literal rendering of the text, suggesting that what the individual binds to himself has its origins at some beginning point alluded to earlier in the text.*

LOGION 104

They said to Yeshua,

"Come,
let's fast
and pray."

He said to them,
"Have I sinned?
Have I been overcome?
No, only when the bridegroom
leaves the bridal chamber,
will it be time to fast and pray."

Academic Translation

They said to Yeshua, "Come, fast and pray today." Yeshua said, "What sin have I committed? In what have I been defeated? When the bridegroom leaves the bridal chamber, then let them fast and pray."

QUESTIONS FOR REFLECTION

1. Why do you suppose those around Yeshua want to fast and pray?
2. What is Yeshua's assumption about this form of practice?
3. What does the image of the bridal chamber mean?
4. What is the experience of being in the bridal chamber?

Personal Reflections

Notes

a. The term **overcome** *is literally "in what have they won over me."*

LOGION 105

Yeshua says,

The one who knows
his true father and mother
will be called
the son of a whore.

Academic Translation

Yeshua said, "The one who knows father and mother will be referred to as the son of a harlot."

QUESTIONS FOR REFLECTION

1. Is this a biographical reference or a purely spiritual teaching?
2. How might it be both?
3. Why would knowing one's (true) father or mother produce such a reaction?
4. What is the advantage of knowing father and mother?

Personal Reflections

Notes

a. The definite article is used both for "the" father and "the" mother, which may indicate not natural, but divine parentage.

LOGION 106

Yeshua says,

When you are able
    to transform
    two into one,
then you too will become
"Son of Humanity,"
and it will be possible
for you to say to a mountain,
"Move," and it will move.

Academic Translation

Yeshua said, "When you make the two one, you will become sons of humanity, and should you speak these words, 'Mountain, move away,' it will move."

QUESTIONS FOR REFLECTION

1. A portion of this saying is familiar from the canonical Gospels. What is not familiar is its linkage to the transformation of two into one, which has been a constant theme in the Gospel of Thomas. Now that you have heard this phraseology a number of times, what does it mean to you?

2. How do you see it linked to becoming "Son of Humanity" (Son of Man in conventional translations)? What is that relationship?

3. Why would such power be attributed to this transformation? What might this form of power have to do with Logion 103?

4. What kind of mountain is being moved? For what purpose?

5. What does it take to transform two into one?

Personal Reflections

Notes

*a. The term **Sons of Humanity** is literally "the sons of the Man."*

LOGION 107

Yeshua says,

The divine Realm
can be compared
to a shepherd
who had one hundred sheep.
One of the finest went astray,
so he left the ninety-nine
and went out searching
for it until he found it.
Troubled he said,
"I longed for you more than
the ninety-nine."

Academic Translation

Yeshua said, "The Kingdom is like a shepherd with one hundred sheep. One of the greatest went astray. He left the ninety-nine and went out searching for it until he discovered it. Having suffered he said, 'I have desired you more than the ninety-nine.'"

QUESTIONS FOR REFLECTION

1. From a form found in the canonical Gospels, this saying is familiar to us. However, something new has been added. What is the addition?
2. What is the shepherd's point of view?
3. What is the shepherd's motivation?
4. What sort of trouble was the shepherd in?
5. What relationship might the shepherd and the sheep have from this point forward?

Personal Reflections

Notes

a. The word **finest** may also be translated as "largest."

b. The term **until he found it** translates the familiar word "seized upon."

c. **Troubled** is the same word used in Logion 57 and may indeed be someone who has "suffered."

d. The term **longed for** can also be translated as "love" or "desire."

LOGION 108

Yeshua says,

Whoever drinks
what flows
from my mouth
will come to be as I am
and I also will come
to be as they are,
so that what is hidden
can become manifest.

**Academic
Translation**

Yeshua said,
"Whoever drinks
from my mouth
will become as I
am, and I also will
become as they are,
and that which is
hidden will appear
to them."

QUESTIONS FOR REFLECTION

1. This saying is full of promise and mystery?
   How do you understand the promise
   made, and its mystery?
2. What is flowing from Yeshua's mouth?
3. What does drinking mean?
4. Does this saying comment on any of the
   immediate sayings preceding this one?
   What might it be teaching?
5. What was hidden that is now manifest?
6. How does it become manifest?

Personal Reflections

Notes

a. The phrase
**what flows
from** *is implied
in the text by the
use of the literal
words, "out of my
mouth." It is
clear from the
text that what is
hidden is
manifest to the
one who drinks,
and does not
simply appear in
general.*

LOGION 109

Yeshua says,

The divine Realm
    is like a man who owned
    a field with treasure
hidden away in it.
Unaware of it he died,
leaving it to his son,
who also knew nothing about it.
After taking possession of the land
the son practically gave
it away for nothing.
But the one who bought
it began plowing
and discovered the treasure,
and immediately started lending
money at interest to
whomever he pleased.

Academic Translation

Yeshua said, "The Kingdom can be compared to had a field in which there was a treasure hidden away. Not knowing about it, after his death he left it to his son. Also unaware, the son took the field and basically gave it away. The one who bought it started plowing and discovered the treasure and began to lend money at interest to whomever he desired."

QUESTIONS FOR REFLECTION

1. Three owners and the treasure lies hidden until the third finds it. Why? What does the third owner do that the other two did not do?
2. How did the first two owners treat the field with the treasure in it? Why would they act in this way?
3. The third owner not only makes the discovery, but he starts using it to his advantage in important ways. If you used this image as a spiritual metaphor, how would you describe his actions?
4. The act of lending at interest in this logion seems to contradict one earlier (95). Is there a difference in these two acts of lending? How do you reconcile them?
5. What does lending mean?

Personal Reflections

Notes

a. The text literally says that the son who inherited the land "gave it away," but in the next line it says the one who bought it began plowing and "seized upon" the treasure. We know, therefore, that the son practically gave it away for nothing, as we might say in colloquial English.

b. In the last line the text literally says that he lent money to "those he loves."

LOGION 110

Yeshua says,

Whoever finds
the cosmos
and becomes rich
must ultimately let the cosmos go.

Academic Translation

Yeshua said, "Let whoever has found the cosmos and become rich abandon the cosmos."

QUESTIONS FOR REFLECTION

1. What is the proper stance toward the cosmos?
2. Is it wrong to benefit from the cosmos?
3. Is everyone rich?
4. Why is letting go so important?
5. What would the effect of letting go be?

Personal Reflections

Notes

a. The original text is written as an imperative in the way the academic version translates it.

LOGION 111

Yeshua says,

Heaven and earth
      will completely disappear
      in your presence,
and the one who lives by means
of the Living One
will not see death,
because,
as Yeshua says,
"The cosmos is not worthy of the one
who discovers the Self."

Academic Translation

Yeshua said, "The heavens and the earth will fade away in your presence. The one who lives from the One who Lives will not look upon death, because as Yeshua says, 'The cosmos is not deserving of the one who finds him (or her) self.'"

Notes

a. This saying is of interest because it appears that Yeshua quotes himself.

b. The term **completely disappear** *is literally "roll up" and* **in your presence** *has an additional term which seems to suggest "outer*

QUESTIONS FOR REFLECTION

1. A new understanding of presence seems to be defined in this saying. What is it?
2. Why and how do heaven and earth disappear in such a presence? What does disappear mean?
3. How is life defined in this logion?
4. Is seeing death different from tasting it or are these cognate metaphors?
5. If they are different, how are they different?
6. Why is the ultimate discovery made in this double logion so crucial?
7. How is the ultimate state like or unlike the current state of humanity?

Personal Reflections

presence," though it is unclear because the word "outer" is often used in Coptic in multiple ways.

c. The phrase **the one who lives by means of the Living One** *is a play on words which appears exactly as the academic version translates it, "The one who lives from the One who Lives..."*

d. The discovery of the **Self** *is emphasized in the text by saying "the one who seizes upon him himself." The word* **worthy** *could also mean "ready for" or "prepared for" as well as* **worthy**.

LOGION 112

Yeshua says,

Wretched is the flesh
that is dependent
upon the soul,
and the soul that is
dependent on the flesh.

**Academic
Translation**

Yeshua said, "Woe
to the flesh that
depends upon the
soul. Woe to the
soul that depends
upon the flesh."

QUESTIONS FOR REFLECTION

1. Why would the dependency described in
   this saying make a person wretched?
2. What does dependency mean?
3. Where do body and soul currently reside in
   the cosmos?
4. What kind of human being does such dependency create?

Personal Reflections

Notes

a. The words
flesh *and* **soul**
*are Greek terms
and used
extensively in the
Christian
Scriptures.*

LOGION 113

His students asked him,

On what day
will the kingdom
arrive?"

"Its coming cannot be perceived
from the outside," he said.
"You cannot say,
'Look, its over there,' or
'No, here it is.'
The Father's realm
is spreading out
across the face of the earth,
and humanity is not able
to perceive it."

Academic Translation

His students said to him, "On which day is the Kingdom coming?" It is not coming by looking on the outside. They cannot say, 'Look, it is on this side,' or 'Behold, it's on that side.' Instead, the Kingdom of the Father is spreading out upon the earth and humanity is not able to see it.

QUESTIONS FOR REFLECTION

1. From the students' questions what do you learn about them?
2. How much do they understand?
3. What kind of seeing is Yeshua talking about?
4. What kind of seeing are his students talking about?
5. Is the Kingdom hidden or not?
6. What keeps humanity from seeing the spread of the Kingdom across the earth?

Personal Reflections

Notes

a. Following the students' question the understanding is that Yeshua answers them, but the normal indicator to that effect is not included in the text. The term **earth** *is literally so, and not "cosmos."*

LOGION 114

Simon Peter said to them all,

Mary should leave us,
for women are not
worthy of this Life."

Yeshua said,
"Then, I myself will lead her,
making her male
if she must become
worthy like you males!
I will transform her
into a living spirit
because any woman changed
in this way
will enter the divine Realm."

This is the Good News
according to Thomas.

Academic Translation

Simon Peter said to them. "Let Mary leave us, for women are not ready for this life." Yeshua said, "Look, I myself will lead her in order to make her male so she becomes a living spirit like you males. For any woman becoming male will go into the Kingdom."

Notes

a. This last saying, which some believe to be an addition to the original text, poses many difficulties for the translator and perhaps the reader as well.

b. On face value Yeshua's answer appears to demean the female students of Yeshua, making them inferior to male students. However, one can easily hear the tone of irony in this text, and if this was indeed the rhetorical mode in which it was spoken (as seems likely when compared with other sayings throughout the Gospel), then the dynamic version is perhaps closer in meaning and tone to Yeshua's original intent.

c. However one translates and interprets this saying, what is clear is that the male students of Yeshua continue to misunderstand both

QUESTIONS FOR REFLECTION

1. In whatever way this last logion is translated, do you think that Yeshua agrees with either the sentiments or solution proposed by Simon Peter?
2. Is Yeshua's answer to Peter reflective of Peter's attitude or Yeshua's?
3. How might Yeshua be helping Peter?
4. What is Yeshua's intention? What does he propose to do?
5. How has this been his intention throughout the entire text?
6. What role does being male or female play in the rest of this text? Are these important categories for Yeshua?
7. What is important to Yeshua, that Mary becomes male or a living Spirit?
8. How does her change relate to the issue of soul and body discussed earlier by Yeshua?
9. Does Yeshua think that Mary will enter the divine Realm?
10. Will you enter it?
11. Is this Gospel "good news"?

Personal Reflections

BIBLIOGRAPHY

Barnhart, Bruno. **The Good Wine: Reading John from the Center**. NY: Paulist Press, 1993.

Cameron, Ron. **The Other Gospels: Non-Canonical Gospel Texts**. Philadelphia: The Westminster Press, 1982.

Clement, Olivier. **The Roots of Christian Mysticism**. Hyde Park, N.Y.: New City, 1993.

Corbin, Henry. **Spiritual Body and Celestial Earth: From Mazdean Iran to Shi'ite Iran** London: I.B. Tauris & Co., 1976.

Corbin, Henry. **The Man of Light in Iranian Sufism**. Boulder & London: Shambhala, 1978.

Crossan, John Dominic. **The Dark Interval**: Towards a Theology of Story. Allen, Texas: Argus Communications, 1975.

Davies, Stevan L. **The Gospel of Thomas and Christian Wisdom**. NY: Seabury, 1983.

Davies, Stevan L. *The Homepage of the Gospel of Thomas* (http://home.epix.net/~miser17/Thomas).

Detweiler, Robert. "What Is a Sacred Text?" **Semeia 31**. Decature, GA: Scholars Press, 1985.

Ernst, Carl W. (Translator) **Ruzbihan Baqli, The Unveiling of Secrets: Diary of a Sufi Master**. Chapel Hill, NC: Parvardigar Press, 1977.

Grant, Robert, M. with David Noel Freedman. **The Secret Sayings of Jesus: According to the Gospel of Thomas**. NY: Collins, 1960.

Grondin, Michael. **Interlinear Coptic/English Thomas Translation** (www.geocities.com/Athens/9058).

Kingsley, Peter. **In the Dark Places of Wisdom**. Inverness, CA: The Golden Sufi Center, 1999.

Leloup, Jean-Yves. **The Gospel of Mary Magdalene**. Rochester, Vermont: Inner Traditions, 2002.

Louth, Andrew. **Discerning the Mystery: An Essay on the Nature of Theology**. Oxford: Clarendon Press, 1983.

Meyer, Marvin. **The Gospel of Thomas: The Hidden Sayings of Jesus**. NY: HarperSanFrancisco, 1992.

Nasr, Seyyed Hossein. **Knowledge and the Sacred**. NY: Crossroad, 1981.

Pagels, Elaine. **Beyond Belief: The Secret Gospel of Thomas**. NY: Random House, 2003.

Palmer, Martin. **The Jesus Sutras: Rediscovering the Lost Scrolls of Taoist Christianity**. NY: Ballantine Publishing, 2001.

Patterson, Stephen J. **The Gospel of Thomas and Jesus**. Sonoma, CA: Polebridge Press, 1993.

Patterson, Stephen J., James M. Robinson, and Hans-Gebhard Bethage. **The Fifth Gospel: The Gospel of Thomas Comes of Age**. Harrisburg, PA: Trinity Press International, 1998.

Ricoeur, Paul. **Interpretation Theory**: Discourse and the Surplus of Meaning. Fort Worth, Texas: The Texas Christian University Press, 1976.

Ricoeur, Paul. **Essays on Biblical Interpretation**. Philadelphia: Fortress Press, 1980.

Robinson, James M., and Marvin W. Meyer (Editors). **The Nag Hammadi Library in English**. NY: Harper and Row, 1988.

Sanders, James A. **Torah and Canon**. Philadelphia: Fortress Press, 1972.

Sanders, James A. **From Sacred Story to Sacred Text**: Canon as Paradigm. Philadelphia: Fortress Press, 1987.

Sells, Michael A. **Mystical Languages of Unsaying**. Chicago and London: The University of Chicago Press, 1994.

Sheppard, Gerad T. **Wisdom as a Hermeneutical Construct**. N.Y.: Walter De Gruyter, 1980.

Sherrard, Philip. **Human Image, World Image: The Death and Resurrection of Sacred Cosmology**. Ipswich, U.K.: Golgonooza Press, 1992.

Sherrard, Philip. **Christianity: Lineaments of a Sacred Tradition**. Brookline, MA: Holy Cross Orthodox Press, 1998.

Shayegan, Daryush. Introduction to **The Green Sea of Heaven: Fifty Ghazals from the Diwan of Hafiz** (by Elizabeth T. Gray). Ashland, Oregon: White Cloud Press, 1995.

Thunberg, Lars. **Microcosm and Mediator: The Theological Anthropology of Maximus the Confessor**. Ejnar Munksgaard Copenhagen: C.W. K. Gleerup Lund, 1965.

Valantasis, Richard. **The Gospel of Thomas**. London and New York: Routledge, 1997.

Von Rad, Gerhard. **Wisdom in Israel**. Nashville: Abingdon Press, 1972.

Warnke, Georgia. **Gadamer: Hermeneutics, Tradition and Reason**. Stanford: Stanford University Press, 1987.

INDEX